Chopsticks

Tigers

&

Chips

Bien Kee-Yeow

Chopsticks, Tigers & Chips
Bien Kee-Yeow

Paperback Edition First Published in Great Britain
in 2015 by aSys Publishing

eBook Edition First Published in Great Britain
in 2015 by aSys Publishing

Copyright © Bien Kee-Yeow

All rights reserved.

No part of this document may be reproduced or transmitted in any form or by any means, electronic, mechanical, photocopying, recording, or otherwise, without prior written permission of the Author.

ISBN: 978-0-9930718-9-8

aSys Publishing
http://www.asys-publishing.co.uk

Acknowledgements

谢谢你
Thank You

Chia Mai Eng, Nicola Mackin, Benjamin Smith, Michelle Bailey for the editing, formatting, cover design and photography respectively.

Table of Contents

Sugarcane Roots 1

The First Three Chords 6

First Date with Teacher Judy 26

Touchdown London 31

Up North of England 35

Oh To Be in England! 48

Another Brick in the Wall 69

Have Guitar Will Travel 74

Wonderful World Wide Web 78

Going Gigs Hunting 81

Smile, you are a CCTV Star! 89

Happy Together 95

Shout Out Loud! 99

We Can Work It Out 104

Best things in life are free 119

Getting It Going 122

How to speak English Chinese style! 129

Allreet Now & Jolly Good 136

Mix & Match	149
Keep On Running	193
Speaking Words of Wisdom	198
Not on my Wedding Day	200
Gigs Gallery	207
Top Ten List	219
International Buskers	231
The English Language	232
Con Te Partiro	235

Prologue

At first glance the title of my book may suggest a cookery book mixed with jungle safari. Chopsticks, Tigers & Chips is not too far off from being a book of ingredients and adventures.

The ingredients are of the human kind, where as Musician and Artistes Agent, I had to gather different personalities with varied musical backgrounds (some who could not stand the sight of the other) and mashed them together, to produce, hopefully, a band of happy smiling and ready to play musicians.

Living in England as a Foreigner has been educational and intriguing!

Switching on the BBC News to hear the latest happenings or going out to hear different accents being banded about in the streets of English towns and villages are all new experiences.

It is also interesting to look at the English way of life through a cross cultural perspective.

Living in a foreign land makes you feel more aware of your culture, origin and ethnicity. Retracing the very bold steps my Grandparents took, leaving behind their homeland China to begin a new life in British Singapore and Malaya, I began to realise all the sacrifices and hard work they made to secure a better future for their children.

What tremendous act of love!

My research into the roots of my ancestors led me back to the year 1644 in Imperial China and their adventures from North China to Fujian in South China, fleeing the Manchu Army, after the fall of the Ming Imperial Court. My forefathers took a big leap of faith in 1826, when they boarded a merchant ship to a new land -the New Nanyang of British ruled Singapore.

In later years my Grandparents moved across to British Colony of Malaya - the thick tropical jungles then crawling with malayan tigers. They, like so many early pioneers, left their beloved China with only hopes and dreams of a better life -in the pockets of their rugged trousers. After independence from Britain, the first Prime

Ministers of Singapore, Lee Kuan Yew and Tunku Abdul Rahman of Malaya respectively, turned and translated aspirations into reality.

Continuing their pioneering spirit in the land of Fish & Chips, England, I hope to make their sacrifices worthwhile- by being successful in a foreign land.

This is my first book, expressed in my own words and written based on real life-experiences.

I hope you will enjoy reading the book; which is peppered with a few anecdotes, and seeing the English and in the wider context, the British way of life as an outsider looking in.

Grab an apple, put your feet up and happy reading!

Y.B Kee-Yeow

bienkee@yahoo.com

Sugarcane Roots

'Never ever forget this and the roots of your forefathers,' my Father said to me, as he thrust a piece of sugar cane stalk into the palms of my hands. As a young boy of five, I have always enjoyed listening to stories told by my Father especially about his large family of brothers and sisters. He had nine brothers and two sisters – a united eleven family team, but not one of them has ever kicked a football!

They were all too busy trying to find three square meals a day to feed themselves and their families.

'See this sugar cane stalk?' he stared at me with a serious look on his face. 'This is me, this is you.'

He started by recalling the year 1644 that witnessed the fall of the Ming Dynasty that ruled China for 276 year since 1368. The victorious Manchus have driven the Imperial Ming Family and its loyalist army from Beijing to the safe havens of South China. The port of Amoy or today known as Xiamen became their outpost and refuge.

Pushing southwards too were the vicious Manchu Army. In the Lunar Chinese New Year of 1646, they were approaching the Fujian province in the South.

A large ethnic minority group of the peasant population who were of the Hokkien Clan, quickly took refuge in the sugar cane plantations to escape being massacred by the invaders.

They stayed hidden throughout the start of the Chinese New Year and on the ninth day, the Hokkien Clan emerged, after the invading Manchu army moved on to the city of ZhangZhou, where they massacred the Hokkien Clan in large numbers.

Among the lucky survivors that hid in the sugar cane plantations were my ancestors, who believed that it was the Jade Emperor God whom they worshipped who saved them. When they emerged from hiding they had nothing to offer their God, so they grabbed a couple of sugar cane stalks and fell on their knees in homage to 'Yu Huang' the Jade Emperor for their salvation.

Since that fateful day, my Ancestors, the Hokkiens have celebrated Chinese New Year with a pair of sugar cane plants, which must be complete stalks from roots to shoots, to commemorate that historical day.

To this day, the sugar cane is a symbol of good fortune, luck and deliverance for us. At all our Hokkien weddings, the sugar cane plants play an important part of the decorations. They would be placed at the entrance to the house of the bridegroom and also carried in the wedding car and also in the design of the invitation cards. Each Chinese New Year celebration is not complete unless prayers, gifts and food are offered to the Jade Emperor God 'Yu Huang' by the Hokkien people.

The Hokkien Clan is Han Chinese and one of the 56 ethnic groups in China and the ancient Chinese Language contained a number of Hokkien words and phrases used in the Imperial Court.

Due to famine and the wars among the various Warlords in those turbulent periods after the fall of the Ming Dynasty in 1644, there began a large scale migration to other lands in the Far East of South East Asia.

In trying to trace back the steps my Grandparents and their relatives took to get to the new British Colony of Singapore and Malaya, I had to rely on research materials available on Chinese Coolie Emigration by writers connected with the London School of Economics and Political Science and other sources on the internet and talking to older family members.

Writer, Persia Crawford Campbell's research book has an excellent account of the indentured system - a form of veiled slave trade, during British Empire era.

After the founding of Singapore by Sir Stamford Raffles in 1819, the British Colonial Masters were crying out to recruit labourers for their new Colonies in Malaya, India, Singapore and other Crown Territories.

As the abolition of the slave trade was in progress, the indentured labour trade was slowly replacing it.

Some desperate local recruiters in China even kidnapped labourers and shipped them abroad to be sold!

The British Colonists had built up contacts with local Chinese Traders and the Labour Recruiters in the port of Amoy which is called Xiamen today. It was from this very busy ancient seaport that many left China to seek new fortunes abroad. My grandparents were one of them.

Some of these recruiters would even build special barracoons called the 'Pig Pens' in front of their firms. Some potential recruits would be stripped naked and examined for defects, if they don't look too healthy.

They would then be offered an advance, known as 'the credit ticket' for their passage and expenses and upon arrival in Singapore would then be sold for US$ 20 - $24 to foreign planters and tin miners.

Only after this indentured debt plus interest was paid back, would my Grandfather and hundreds like him, be free men!

My Grandfather and his brothers took the opportunity to escape the turmoil and hardship in China to board the merchant ship and set sailed for Singapore, to seek their new fortune abroad. On the perilous journey with his brothers, the merchant ship were full and men packed like sardines on board. Quite a few men died on the trip.

Sailing for days under the hot Eastern Sun, under such harsh conditions, produced and churned out tough men of steel and determination when they arrived at the port of Singapore.

They were HRRTW - Hardened, Rough and Ready to work. My Grandfather and his brothers and those on board were lucky to leave a troubled China. They were indeed very grateful to the British Merchants who gave them the opportunity, to work in a new land.

On arrival in Singapore Island, a proportion of the passengers were selected to work on the island whilst a vast numbers were transferred to tiger - infested Malaya to clear the thick virgin jungles, which were home to lots of wild animal - elephants, wild boars, monkeys, snakes and tigers. Actually, the more dangerous species were the hunters of tigers for their beautiful fur. It was a lucrative trade at that time, especially the crazed demand in the west for their fur for floor rugs or clothings.

Some unlucky ones did not return alive according to tales from my grandfather.

A large numbers were sent to work on the newly open cast tin mines and other new opportunities in local trades and industries, particularly the flourishing rubber tapping in the plantations.

In later years my grandparents and my parents' standard of living began to improved significantly due to their hard work and enterprise.

Growing up within an orderly structured family environment based on the teachings of Confucius, there was a lot of discipline (caning with a rattan stick is common) and also respect for the elders and authority.

We would never dream of talking back to our parents or questioning our elders - even if we think they are wrong. Confucius influence is strong within us and the customs we inherited from our parents and forefathers are evident in our daily living. Those customs and traditions are deeply rooted as is evidenced in the bound feet of my grandmother. Ladies with bound feet are supposed to look more dainty and attractive.

Take the distinct association – the Chopsticks. A pair of chopsticks is more than just a pair of thin, tapered sticks made of wood used to pick up foods.

It goes to the very heart of the Chinese psyche and has great emotional attachment for us and bring us closer to each other especially during daily mealtime.

Our parents picked food for us with it, when we were kids. We learn to be considerate and share food with others with it. The customary way of using the chopsticks to eat rice is to scoop the rice from a small bowl into your mouth and pick your choice of meat or veg with the pair.

At home it has always been chopsticks and bowls and like the forks and knives to the Europeans, it is part of us.

When I discovered the western folk and knife through a friend at his home and liked the easy use of them, he gave a pair to me to take home.

I invited stares of disapproval from my parents and relatives when

I started using them at dinner time, and quickly reverted to the time honoured chopsticks after a few uncomfortable nights around the dining table.

Placing it properly when not using it, teach us not to be offensive - it is a sin in Chinese custom to stick chopsticks at a certain angle into a bowl of rice!

Such a practice is usually carried out at the traditional burial service.

My Chopsticks Roots

Tracing my roots that goes way back to Fujian province in Southern China, from research and facts gathered from relatives has been enlightening and soul searching.

A historian once said you need to know where you come from, to know where you should be heading.

Wise words indeed.

It has been said that an Emigrant would take on jobs the locals would shun or avoid. There is some truth in this, and perhaps it is knowing where you come from and the trials and tribulations your forefathers have been through, that drive one to new adventures with hope, faith and determination.

That same spirit drove my parents, as they did for my grandparents, who left their village in Po Tien, Fujian in Southern China to build a new and better life in British Singapore and Malaya.

I only hope that they will be proud, if I carried on the same spirit in my new journey in the Land of Hope and Glory, England and other newer pastures, in the future.

The First Three Chords

With brother Yew Keong & Guan.

Tarmac road beside us, double up as a football ground.

Sitting under the coconut palm trees shading all five of us from the very hot tropical Malayan Sun, I was totally mesmerized and transfixed with Zaccheus Choo's guitar playing. His four fingers moved with lightning speed as he changed from one chord to the next - smiling as he did so effortlessly. He taught us how to sing Amazing Grace and told us background stories of a couple of gospel songs and played some instrumentals from the British band, The Shadows and a selection of jazz numbers.

We were a group of five good friends, all thirteen years of age, very easy to please, all very wide eyed and hero worshippers. Guru Zak was our idol and hero.

A family friend Guru Zak, as he was popularly known was the local Hank Marvin in our town, except that he does not wear spectacles - a Marvin trademark. A soft drinks and sweets salesman by trade, he promoted the Coca Cola brand and a local concoction that went by the comical, unique, funky sounding and happy brand name of 'Kickapoo' Oh how we as kids truly love our daily Kickapoo - a fizzy, yellowish aerated water drink. And what a name for a drink!

Like Kickapoo, which has the 'oomph' factor, there was never a dull or quiet moment when Guru Zak was around. He had a great presence in abundance and in bucket loads. A tall six footer giant towering over us - his skinny insignificant, curious wide eyed scrawny hero worshippers. He was very articulate, loud and he had what we know later to be known as 'charisma.' What we all found interesting and enjoyable was his slightly off the key singing, his slightly out of tune guitar playing and his colourful and friendly personality.

Being curious early teenagers, we were fascinated by his gospel stories and 'the meaning of life' tales he would share with us. To us, Guru Zach came across as a very pious and religious man and his main mission in life, as he put it, was to 'convert and save as many lost lives as possible to the faith'.

Given a chance, he would have converted my pet dog Chuck - if only Chuck would sit quietly to listen to his 'under the stars' sermon.

I later discovered, like his namesake in the good book that he likes climbing up trees for bird watching - the fly by birds with wings and also the kind of birds that could walk and talk on the ground, as in the British slang - meaning girls.

Watching Guru Zak's guitar playing had a major profound effect on me that afternoon under the coconut trees. I felt I have found something interesting to take up as a hobby beside coming to meet my friends each weekend to feed peanuts to the monkeys and watched them climbing up the coconuts trees and shake and pluck the fruits and throw the coconuts to the ground. It was really fun to watch the monkeys in action! That night when I got home, I could not help but kept thinking about Guru Zak's guitar rendering.

Guru's performance excited me and I was eager to learn how to play the instrument, however long it takes.

I was eleven years old then, and one of my passion was playing football daily with my neighbours and childhood friends, Francis and Bernard Soo.

Our grand football field that stretched from the first house to the end of the terraced row was the narrow tar-surfaced road right in front of our terraced houses. Our houses literally faces each other and we could almost see into each other spaces, to see what was happening on a daily basis. I once saw Francis having a trashing from his strict Mother–a lovely very disciplined lady, who I call Aunty. Francis was disciplined with the cane for being involved in a street fight.

It is also quite a common practice back home to use the cane to discipline children, even till this day

Francis's fight with a neighbour was over a girl with a very fair complexion. It was trendy to have fair skin as it is considered pretty and dainty. Our girls prefer to stay indoor to get a fair complexion as compared to their counterparts in Europe, who like to bask in the sun to get a tan. Majority of our girls in the Far East go out using umbrellas to shield them from the sun.

Umbrellas sell really well in our part of the world!

Our neighbourhood had an air of friendliness and a kind relaxed way of life. We hardly lock our doors. It was very safe. Beside we have nothing much in the house to take anyway - a few chairs, tables, two table lamps, a radio, some mosquito nets, books, cut out toys from borrowed magazines. The most expensive item in the house was the black and white television in the living room. And of course, Chuck, our adorable pet dog.

Besides kicking football to past the time and also for exercise purposes, we also played marbles, sepak raga, which is a local Malayan rattan ball game, ping pong, basketball and catching and keeping tiny spiders. We would catch tiny spiders hiding in their leaves from the trees in our nearby forest, and keep them in colourful matchboxes as a personal pet. But in this case, it was a kind of fighting pet. It was at that time, our treasure and hobby. A nearby jungle and forest ensure we got constant supply of the spiders.

The game entails putting a spider on a big banana leaf and let it face an opposing spider. When they meet face to face, there is usually some sort of gentle fighting with their arms and legs for a few second, and the spider that turn away is the loser.

Every Saturday weekend, the kids in the neighbourhood would meet at the corner store, and after proudly showing their pet and precious possession would all gather in a circle, waiting for the competition to start. We could feel the excitement in the air!

There was no computer games, computer, mobile phones or electronic gadgets then.

This is it. Our favourite hobby pre-electronic games era.

Inside our colourful matchbox was our crawly little hero. Our little tiny furry heros, who have all been given their nicknames after our idols, or some famous actors and a few named after teachers we don't really like.

This was our Saturday night fever for all of us - young, freckless and carefree in Singapore and Malaya.

Yes, spider fighting was the rave at that time.

We would all gather round in a circle and place our bets - really a princely small bet, like less than five Malayan cent per fight equivalent to less than a British penny, to see which of our spider would emerge the champion.

It would be a one to one fight.

There is no bloodletting. Just two spiders squaring up to each other and a few mooching about and a gentle fight for a couple of seconds, till the loser turn and run away!

Being an animal lover, I can assure readers that no real physical harm came to our crawling friends. I would not imagine doing this today.

Sliding the matchbox open to take my tiny Harry out when my turn came, I took it and place it gently on a big banana leaf, ready to face its opponent, a fierce looking spider called Wongfei. I think its owner named it after the famous Kung Fu Master at that time, Wong Fei Hong, the Bruce Lee of the sixties.

It is a strong fighting name.

Poor Harry! I thought 'Shall I put him back?' Then I reasoned he won last time, so there is the possibility and chance for Harry to shine again tonight.

One look at Wongfei, my Harry turned round and ran the other direction. One direction actually.

This was one of the many past time activities we had, whilst growing up as kids in sunny Malaya. Coming back to my newly found interest - the guitar. That night, as I tucked myself into bed I started thinking about Guru Zak's finger movements.

Gosh, I thought, how did Guru Zak do that!

The sound of the guitar overwhelms my thoughts and there was this big urge to learn how to play it and I pledged that moment that I will go all out to master the instrument. But first I had to get hold of a guitar.

I was young, impatient and in a hurry!

Being from a family that was struggling where all five of us - all brothers, have to roll out our rattan mattress at night to sleep in the hall and roll them back again in the morning, as we had only two rooms in our home. Getting a guitar seem like a distant dream. I remember cutting out a picture of a guitar from a magazine and looking at it daily. I was like a boy possessed and obsessed!

The next few days and weeks were spent on checking out the music shops and looking at the different guitars on display. As I walked into the guitar shop in Kuala Lumpur, all the shiny and polished up guitars were reflected on the big mirror glass on the wall.

It was heaven to me to see so many guitars on display. Polished and shimmering guitars were shown here, there and everywhere. The Fenders, Gibsons, Hofners, and some German and Continental brands seemed to be saying to me 'Hey, please choose me'

The display and variety of guitars in the shop–both the electric and acoustic guitars were so inviting.

Just looking at them without even able to play a chord was just so tempting! There were so many different brands. I set my eyes for the first time on this blue coloured guitar - that was beckoning to me to pick it up.

As I walked towards it, picked it up and twang the strings, it resonated with a beautiful sound, even though I could not play a note or a chord. Holding the guitar in my hands, it felt so right and so good.

An hour later, I walked out of the shop with only a guitar chords book in my hand but I was determined to come back for the guitar when I have saved enough.

Lady Luck smiled on me one day, in the form of a school teacher, Miss. Judy (not her real name, to protect her identity, as will be explained in Chapter 2) who was our music teacher at Bukit Bintang primary school in Petaling Jaya.

The First Three Chords

Seeing how interested I was in the instrument, Miss Judy very kindly allowed me to borrow and take her guitar home for a month. It was a brownish colour guitar with some flowery design and she showed me a bamboo pipe for tuning the instrument.

It was a guitar tuner which was very classic and the forerunner of the modern electronic tuner - you blow into each of the six holes echoing the various keys to tune.

Thanking her, I promised I would take good care of the guitar and will play her a tune when I have learnt my first song.

Walking home back from school with my neighbour and childhood friends, the Soo Brothers, I was the happiest teenager on earth and there was a burning desire to play the guitar straight away. The first thing I did when I got home, was to open the guitar chord book I purchased weeks earlier. Opening the first page, 'Viola' there were the diagrams of all the finger placings for all the different chords. It makes learning chords easier.

Today with the internet and the various video clips on Youtube, so many beginners and learners around the globe can see and learn much quicker.

My brother's friend, Vincent Raj, a guitarist also gave me some tips previously, he said, 'Learn the first three chords, A, D and E first, and once you are confident of it, then progress to other chords later' he advised.

As I started to place my three little fingers on the guitar second fret to indicate where the A chord placing should be, I heard a shout from outside of my house. My football teammates and neighbourhood pals, Bernard and Francis started calling for me to come out to play, which was one of our usual pastime activities in the evening.

For the first time I did not join them, as I was too engrossed in my new found hobby. As days go by I started to stay in more and more and stayed away from joining in the game. It was a start to learning new songs and chords and listening to singers and groups from England and America over the radio was very useful and interesting.

Hearing the Beatles 'Please Please Me' over the radio was just awesome, even if hearing it for the very first time years after it was first released in England.

Who are they?

Where do they come from?

I was curious and later finding out they were from England, and that they were a guitar band inspired me more!

For a thirteen year old, it was such a joy strumming the guitar, even if it is was only just one chord!

I learned through the hard way that for beginners, it always help to start off with nylon strings on an acoustic guitar as compared to steel strings guitar. It is much gentler on the fingers.

The bleeding on my little fingers is a good lesson.

After six hours of practicing the same three chords A, D and E, it was time for bed. Little did I realize all those hours have passed by and I have missed my dinner, but the strange thing is, I wasn't hungry, in fact I was full and full of happiness that at last, I have learnt those essential chords.

The next step is to learn a song to play for Miss Judy, when I return the guitar in a couple of weeks.

The next morning was a glorious sunny Saturday and after breakfast, I took out my new found friend and started practicing again.

As I was going through the repetitive finger movement of the chords, a Country and Western cowboy song 'Red River Valley' that I often hear on the local Rediffusion Radio Station came to mind and it became the first song that I learnt and planned to play for Miss Judy.

'From this Valley they say you are going,
We will miss your bright eyes and sweet smile,
For they say you are taking the sunshine
That brightens our pathway a while'

As I strummed the chord of A and tried to match the remaining chords to the song of Red River Valley, I was wondering when the next chord will and should take place. Through trials and errors, and after another few hours of torturous fret-board fingering and testing, where one of my fingers bled from the constant pressing on the very hard steel guitar strings, the tune & chords started to fall into place and the tune finally came out.

Although I was not sure with my progress, I was pleased with the way my guitar playing was shaping up and was determined that I shall play 'Red River Valley' for my Teacher, Miss. Judy, in a couple of weeks, when returning back her guitar.

The School Concert –Shaking All Over!

A couple of months later, Miss. Judy was put in charge of organizing the school annual music concert and was looking to put a group of us on stage.

'I was so impressed with the way you so quickly learn and play the guitar, and I think you should be in the group' she said looking straight at me and waiting for my reaction.

'Me, with a guitar on the stage?' I responded, looking puzzled and not overtly excited at the prospect of making a right fool of myself in front of the whole school, classmates and my parents.

I must have impressed her enough with my three chords wonder of 'Red River Valley'.

'Yes, you with a guitar on stage, with another boy, Imbran and yes you can do it, I know you can' she shot back.

'OK then, if you said so' I began sounding a bit more confident after hearing Miss. Judy's compliments.

'I shall get Mr. Han, the guitar teacher to help you out and all will be fine' she continued with some assurance.

A few days later, Imbran and I started practicing the four songs with the group of ten singers. Two of the songs were Indonesian folk songs, 'Bangawan Solo' and 'Widuri' the other two songs were country and western

'Oh Susanna' and 'Red River Valley' which were regularly sung in school and on the local radio station.

Agreeing to give it a try, partly to please Miss. Judy and wanting to keep my favoured position with her, and being Teacher's pet breeds envy and jealously envied by others, especially spoilt brat, Dennis Fong. Dennis own motto seem to be 'Why can't I, be the Teacher's pet instead of that sissy type fellow.'

He was referring to me - the quiet goody goody type.

Being the favoured and the quietest boy in class has its backlash time and a target for boys from the big bully Dennis. He was rather large for his age and had a very serious look all the time!

The idea of being in a group and performing in front of a live audience got me really excited.

I was delighted that at long last, all those long hours spent in my bedroom, practicing on the guitar whilst others were out kicking a ball has paid off.

This invitation to perform for the school came out of the blue and I was now more determined to do well.

I rushed home excitedly to tell my parents the good news. All those sore fingers pressing on the strings, the patience and determination in the learning to play an instrument has borne fruits. Patience is a virtue?

I soon learn religiously all the right chords to all the four songs, guided by and under the expert hands of our guitar teacher, Mr. TT Han, who is actually a Spanish guitar player and is left handed.

A guitar maestro, the gift he had was the ability to flip a normal right hand type guitar and play it straight away - looking like it is an upside down movement. Many more rehearsals followed and soon the day came for all of us to perform in front of an audience made up of staff, pupils, parents and invited guests.

D-day is here and we are all assembled in a waiting room with Teacher Miss. Judy.

Twiddling our thumbs and with the heavy breathing making the round, all fourteen of us were very anxious and were trembling with fear.

The reassuring figure of Miss. Judy pepped us up, she spoke and got us all ready. 'Go out there and put on a good show' she commanded.

Not one of us - male virgins, have ever been on stage in our lives and the thought of facing the whole school was just sheer terror! Worst was yet to come.

We then got word that the Headmistress, Mrs. Leong and most feared of the pack, Discipline Tiger, Mr Kok who had the authority to cane us, are now seated right in the front row. Now this is fear personified and fear doubled! I can hear an echo 'Run for your life now!'

We are now wetting in our pants and this shook us up. Our well ironed white shirts tucked under our short panes now started to display a beautiful sweat design under our arm pits, and there was a sudden rush to the toilet by a few. But we do look splendid with an elegant black dinner bow tie, as shown in the photograph in this section of the book.

One of us actually had breathing problems and he nearly passed out but luckily recovered in time. Thanks to our locally made Tiger palm rub ointment - rubbed into his nose.

As our group name was announced, Judy ushered us on to the stage. Looking at what look like a thousand people in a stadium, all fixing their stares at you, I was soon trembling and very quickly froze and totally forgot all the chords to the first number and it was Imbran, the other guitarist who rescued me. Bless him! He was from Indonesia and knew the Indonesian folk song 'Bangawan Solo' very well.

I soon gained back my composure and confidence (and the temporary loss of memory) and was winging it to the end of the set, even though my hot legs in those short hot panes could not hide my shivers!

Luckily it all went well, and the audience gave us a big round of loud thunderous applause! The Headmistress, Mrs. Leong, the Discipline Tiger, Mr. Kok, Miss. Judy and Mr. T. Han were all truly pleased, judging from the looks on their happy faces and giving us the thumbs up.

Personally, I would not have done it without the loan of the guitar by Miss Judy and the expert 'guiding left hand' of Mr. T.T. Han, the guitar maestro.

It was a really good learning journey for all those involved in the show especially for us – the green horns.

Whilst we congratulated ourselves after the concert, we all felt a tinge of sadness knowing this is the last concert, before we all leave primary school.

Our primary school year starts at 8 years old. That is why we look rather large in our last primary year at 13 years old in the school concert photograph.

Tears flowed freely and we hugged and sign each other personal autograph books.

We bade farewell to all we know and have grown up with all through the years of our primary school life Teachers, Schoolmates, Classmates and the much loved and respected Headmistress, Mrs. Leong. I said a special thank you and goodbye to Miss. Judy.

There were no kisses - just some handshakes and smiles and a bit of a tear. I did give her a small gift.

I did winked at her as well, as we said our last goodbye and she was amused at my cheeky action.

'Well done, you all did us proud and do keep in touch. You never know when we all will meet again.' Miss Judy said to all of us, as we gathered for a group photograph.

A few calls of 'Smile!' and a couple of clicks of the photographer's camera ended one of many poignant and memorable moments in our primary school life.

Imbran & I accompanying Bukit Bintang Primary School Choir
Looks like we all have pairs of matchsticks pin legs!

Terry Thaddeus – The Guitar Legend

After leaving primary school and encouraged by the success of the concert performance, I began to take a keener interest in guitar playing and started to go out watching bands performing.

One of the bands that caught my attention was a group named The Teenage Hunters in a girl's school called the Assunta School in Petaling Jaya, a satellite town just on the outskirt of Kuala Lumpur.

They were a four piece unit consisting of a drummer and three guitarists.

The loud screams and the warm applause from the audience confirmed the popularity of the band. They were just superb! The lead guitarist of the band was a lanky, tall Indian gentleman, Terry Thaddeus.

It would be a couple of years later that our paths crossed - at an audition for a guitarist for his brother's pop group, The Junior Hunters.

I was most pleased and fortunate to have met Asia and Malaysia top musician guitarist, Terry Thaddeus of The Teenage Hunters fame. He had a great impact on me and on so many musicians in Malaysia and Singapore.

The influencing figure behind Terry's success and his enduring legacy, in this part of South East Asia music scene was his late father.

Affectionately called Uncle Thaddeus, he guided and encouraged Terry from a young teenage age to take up guitar playing and had him practice for hours in their Bangsar home in Kuala Lumpur. The house was a mecca in the early sixties with lots of musicians stopping by from all over South East Asia to visit Terry or have a jam session.

It was always followed by a nice plate of homemade curry and tea by his lovely mum and the jam session would start all over again.

Uncle and Auntie Thaddeus made sure Terry had all the latest and best band gear.

There were the Vox and Fender amplifiers and guitars and the Ludwig drumset, popularized by the Beatles Ringo Starr.

They were the envy of the musicians in town. The sound that

echoed through Terry's guitar was sweet and was a fitting testimony to him - he was Terry fic!

Terry had talent in abundance and a very good ear for music and in later years became a producer. His jingles on radio advertising won awards for creativity.

A lot of guitarists in Singapore and Malaysia were influenced by him and his style of playing, and he was proclaimed as the Jimi Hendrix of the Far East.

Moving around with him, I have seen how dedicated he was to his craft. He personify what a really good guitarist should be and he would be very encouraging to all the budding musicians he meets. I was blessed to have been guided by him and developed a kind of brotherly relationship with him and his younger brothers.

Terry's Teenage Hunters was the most sought after and top Band in the region in the sixties - they were the 'Numero Uno' in Malaysia and Singapore.

The group had a top hit record with the EMI label recording of 'Goin' Places' composed by Terry and wherever they play, it was the most requested number of the evening. Terry was totally devoted to his guitar craft and spend many hours in his home trying out new instruments, practicing and experimenting with different sounds and also with a band of different musicians. A host of famous musicians have passed through the doors of the Thaddeus LLN home in Kuala Lumpur, like The Strollers and Singapore's top group, The Quest.

The Junior Hunters would always be the warming up and opening act for The Teenage Hunters shows all over the country in Malaysia and Singapore. One of their regular weekend residency spot was in Jackies Disco. Jackies was situated along Ampang Road, in Kuala Lumpur. The Sunday T-dance event attracted a lot of young, trendy yuppie professionals and the Expatriate community, majority of them British and Americans.

A number of English expatriates brought vinyl records from UK and USA to play at the disco.

Lots of local Musicians look forward to the latest of these records brought by the Expats at the Club, as it can take months before such newly released records reach our shores. There were the latest from the stable of EMI, Decca and American labels too. Among the groups were The Beatles, Rolling Stones, Kinks, Jimi Hendrix, Santana, Simon and Garfunkel, Creedence Clearwater Revival, Beach Boys, Procul Harum etc.

Just watching Terry play the guitar was so exciting and inspirational - he was nicknamed the Jimi Hendrix of the Far East. In observing his style of playing, one could learn so much more, being there rather than from a book and is like a free practical guitar lessons

We all look up to our peers in whatever field of interest to reach their standards and Terry Thaddeus was the benchmark for many up and coming guitarist. He makes the guitar come alive and play with a lot of passion

Terry Thaddeus & The Teenage Hunters

Another icon of Malaysia-Singapore pop music industry and who had a large influence in the local pop music scene is Jerry Ventura. Whilst still in primary school he formed a band with his school mates. The band, The Falcons became a household name in the region and had a No.1 hit with the instrumental 'Baby Elephant Walk' on the EMI label. Jerry is a multi-talented instrumentalist and is the bass /saxophone player in the Falcons.

I was fortunate to have had the privilege of being a member of The Falcons, as a stand-in, when their lead guitarist was unavailable.

Today, after having performed over a thousand gigs in various venues in Singapore, Malaysia, Italy and in the UK, I can see the wisdom of the words and sayings of Chinese Philosopher, Confucius. A journey of a thousand miles does indeed begin with the first step.

For Musicians it begin with the First Three Chords. Learning and mastering the essential first three, will lead to other more interesting chords - those power chords! It took me hours to master the basic three chords and it was a struggle at first to try to change the guitar keys in a smooth way. It does hurt at first but gets easier later.

Most Rock n' Roll songs are based on the winning structure three chords, be it C, F G or A, D, E.

Status Quo rocked the music world using the same formula. There are a hundred of three chords songs.

The Rhythm is infectious and once it starts, it is hard to stop it. It can go on and on, with a dancing crowd.

Listed below are a selection of a variety of popular songs based on the magical three chords or less:

- » Amazing Grace – John Newton
- » Alberta – Eric Clapton
- » All Along The Watchtower – Jimi Hendrix
- » All Shook Up – Elvis Presley
- » Bad Moon Rising – Creedence Clearwater Revival
- » Ballad of John and Yoko – John Lennon & Yoko
- » Bachelor Boy – Cliff Richard
- » Be-Bop-A-Lula – Gene Vincent
- » Blowin' In the Wind – Bob Dylan
- » Blue Moon of Kentucky – Roy Acuff
- » Blue Suede Shoes – Carl Perkins
- » Bye Bye Love – Everly Brothers

The First Three Chords

- Caroline – Status Quo
- Chasing Cars – Snow Patrol
- Do Wah Diddy Diddy – Manfred Mann
- Donna – Ritchie Valens
- Evil Ways - Santana
- Five Hundred Miles – The Journeymen
- Folsom Prison Blues – Johnny Cash
- Get Back –The Beatles
- Guantanamera – Jose Feliciano
- Great Balls of Fire – Jerry Lee Lewis
- Green Green Grass of Home –Tom Jones
- Hey Good Looking – Hank Williams
- I Can Stop Loving You – Ray Charles
- I Walk The Line – Johnny Cash
- If I Had a Hammer – Trini Lopez
- Itsy, Bitsy, Teeny, Weeny, Yellow Polka, Dot Bikini by Brian Hyland
- Jailhouse Rock – Elvis Presley
- Jambalaya – Hank Williams
- Johnny B. Goode – Chuck Berry
- Joy to The World –Andy Williams
- Kansas City – Wilbert Harrison
- King Of The Road - Roger Miller
- La Bamba – Trini Lopez
- Leaving on a Jetplane – The Carpenters
- Long Tall Sally – Little Richard

- Lucille – B.B. King
- Move It – Cliff Richard and the Shadows
- Mony Mony – Tommy James & The Schondells
- Midnight Special – Dave Cutrell
- Oh! Susanna – Stephen Foster
- Obla Di Obla Da – The Beatles
- Old Time Rock n'Roll – Bob Seeger
- Que Sera Sera – Doris Day
- Rave On – Buddy Holly
- Red River Valley – Bob Nolan & Sons of the Pioneers
- Red Red Wine – Bob Marley
- Ring of Fire – Johnny Cash
- Rockin' All Over The World – Status Quo
- Rockin' Robin – Bobby Day
- Rudolph The Red Nose Reindeer – Johnny Marks
- Satisfaction – The Rolling Stones
- Shake, Rattle and Roll – Bill Haley & his Comets
- Singing The Blues – Guy Mitchell
- Sloop John B – The Beach Boys
- Save The Last Dance For Me – The Drifters
- Sex On Fire – Kings of Leon
- Stir It Up – Bob Marley
- Surfin' USA – The Beach Boys
- Sweet Home Chicago – Blues Brothers
- Tambourine Man – Bob Dylan
- Teddy Bear – Elvis Presley

- » That's All Right Mama – Arthur Crudup
- » The Gambler –Kenny Rogers
- » This Land is Your Land – Woody Guthrie
- » Tutti Frutti – Little Richard
- » Twist & Shout – The Beatles
- » Walk of Life – Dire Straits
- » Walking The Dog – Rufus Thomas
- » What I'd Say – Ray Charles
- » Where Have All The Flowers Gone – Pete Seeger
- » Wild Thing – The Troggs
- » Wolly Bully – Sam the Sham & The Pharaohs
- » Yellow Submarine – Ringo Starr
- » You Are My Sunshine – Pine Ridge Boys

The three chords is especially useful for those who don't read notes and want to move on in a faster pace and progress by the 'play by ear' method.

It is the quickest way to start to play and get going.

The most prevalent of the three-chord song is the simple twelve bar blues used in blues and rock and roll. Paul McCartney and John Lennon wrote some of their most popular hits based on three chords too and based on personal feelings and life experiences.

One important asset is, you do need a pair of good ears to begin. Those three chords I learned were the first three steps to music heaven and led to the opening of new opportunities and also making new friends all over the world - or in a word 'Rocking all over the world'.

The history of the guitar can be traced back to over 4,000 years. An Egyptian singer, Har-Mose was buried with his tanbur, close to the tomb of his employer, Sen-Mut who was the architect to Queen Hatshepsut, crowned in 1503 BCE. The tanbur is indeed the oldest preserved guitar-like instrument and is the ultimate vintage guitar!

The guitar is such a lovely companion. It is easy to carry about has a great acoustic sound (can double up as a drum, as most Spanish guitarist will demonstrate this method of strum and beat in their playing) and wonderful to entertain at campfires and parties. To some, being able to strum and play the guitar does have its advantage of attracting the attention of the people being entertained, particularly the girls!

I never took up guitar playing to impress anyone or the girls. It was just the love of the twang and vibes of the instrument and the fact that it is so portable, one can take it anywhere in the bed, play it while watching television, on the train, in the car, on the bus, in the park or on the beach.

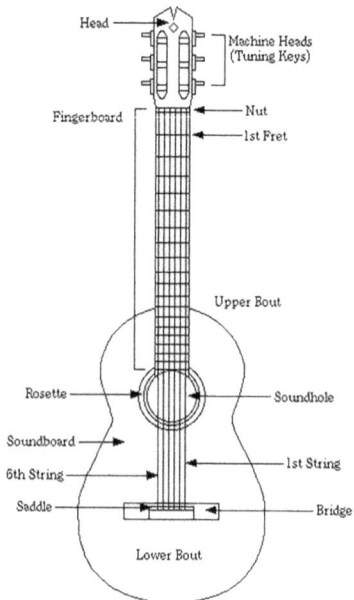

The Hikers

Some of the bands I have played with in the early years from 1972.

The first band, The Hikers had a regular Saturday spot at the home of the bassist.

The Raiders 3 Plus One

We were so excited being in a band and the sheer love of it meant we played almost non-stop for free

The friends and people who came loved it. They danced in the living room on the cement floor and many couples kept asking us to extend a song, particularly slow numbers.

This gave them a chance to hold and embraced their female partners very very closely and tightly!

Their favourite was 'When The Girl In Your Arms' by Cliff Richard.

Freedom Xpression

At one point we repeated the song six times, as that was the only slow number we knew! The Guys hugging their partners loved it !

First Date with Teacher Judy

To this day, I cannot believe that my very first date with the opposite sex was with a school teacher. She was twenty five years old and I was thirteen. She was my form and music teacher.

My childhood friend and classmate Francis also had a crush on Miss Judy too (not her real name, to protect her identity) She was an attractive slim and a stylish lady. Majority would say she is classy. Most of the boys in the class would be fighting to win her attention, as soon as she walks into the room, to take us for drama and music class.

My date with Miss Judy happened on a school sports day held in mid-morning attended by the parents and members of the general public. It was a fine sunny day and lots of games and competitions were organised to showcase the school sports talent among the pupils.

Earlier in the week we had some rehearsals and all went well and everyone was looking forward to the big event that took place once a year.

I was part of a six member bicycle race team. Each cyclist was required to complete one full round in the field race, and then pass on the baton to the next member waiting at the end of the finishing line.

In the final lap round, I was nearing the finishing line, when another cyclist came too close and accidently knocked me down to the ground. I had various bruises and cuts to my feet and hands. Miss Judy quickly came to my rescue.

She was the first Teacher to reach me and come to my aid with some bandages, as I had a large wound in my left arm and bruises all over my body. I was in a state of shock and all shook up!

First Date with Teacher Judy

Helping me up on my feet, and seeing the cuts and bruises on my legs and hands, she appeared concern for me, and said that she would ask the Headmistress for permission to take me to the clinic, in the old part of the town, about five miles away from the school.

Permission granted, we were soon heading into town in Miss Judy's pink coloured Volkswagen car. You can see it from miles! Sex on Wheels!

After being given a good examination (by the Doctor) and being treated by the Doctor, we stepped outside the clinic which was facing a cinema - The Majestic. I thanked her for taking me to the clinic for emergency treatment and for her care and kindness all these while. Walking to her car affectionately called Pinky Herbie, we both started looking at the direction of the cinema and both our eyes were fixed on the huge picture of the King himself, yes Elvis, Presley on the billboard of the cinema building.

I remarked how I was a fan of Elvis Presley and Ms Judy also confessed he was her idol too!

'That makes two Elvis fans' I remarked.

Ahha! A Huckleberry! I thought to myself.

'Yes, indeed. I am a huge fan of his' she said, curling her lips, (well at least, that was what I was imagining her gesture of faithfulness to the King of Rock n' Roll, at that moment in time ... a aha aha ! Elvis is in the building moment!

And then to my total amazement, she turned to me and asked me in a very nice, soft and friendly tone.

'Would you like to go and see the show?'

I could not believe what I was hearing.

Here I was, all shook up and all my arm bandaged up, cut on the lips with dried blood, not looking good and being asked out on my first movie date, and by my class Drama and Music Teacher!

I never imagine my first date would turned out like this –in a movie with my Teacher!

It was like a dream! How good can fairy tale be for a teenager, who has never been out on a date, simply because I was terribly shy in class (usually always keeping a low profile, sitting behind a big built boy and avoiding eye contact with any Teachers, in case they call my name out to read during lessons.

I used to have a high voice and was rather embarrassed to read in class especially during Literature Class. Now, all of a sudden in wonderland I am being asked by my Teacher to go on a movie date! It is like a wet dream!

'Yes, that would be really wonderful, Thank you' I replied enthusiastically.

I think she felt sorry for me and thought perhaps a treat to the movie, starring our favourite star/singer would do wonders for me and cheer me up, after the ugly incident.

We both really enjoyed the movie - it was a beautiful innocent experience for us – there was no hand holding in the dark or anything that was inappropriate. I must admit that I was tempted to hold her hands, when the lights dimmed and the whole hall went into darkness and only the projector lights shone on, past all the heads of the audience.

We were seated right in the back row of the movie. Aha!

Many years later, we both met at a school reunion party for ex-pupils and teachers at our Alma Mater. (alma mater the Latin phrase which literally means 'nourishing mother' - it refers to the school or college a person has attended) I guess she was mothering me then and was concern about my welfare.

Recalling my misadventure incident at sports day, the visit to the clinic and how the two of us ended up in a cinema, watching an Elvis movie, we both laughed it off as something totally hilarious and a memorable experience for both of us! Neither of us knew what was actually happening until the movie was over.

Teacher taking young pupil to a movie is not a common thing back home but it is not a crime or would make headlines or raise eyebrows.

In England, this would indeed be a major cause of concern if it were to happen in this day and age. It would make front page news

The Police & Child protection team would soon be knocking on her door, and circling all over her, and taking her in for questioning, and very likely, possible prosecution against an adult Teacher dating a 13 year old pupil.

This would have been a major news splash in the national newspapers!

Imagine the headline. . . . 'Teacher enticed 13 year old pupil and brought him to an Elvis movie, where they munch on popcorns, sitting in the back row of a movie.'

This item would be in every papers hot headlines and juicy news storyline in the United Kingdom.

The UK press would have a field day and will tear the Teacher and pupil into pieces with hot gossips.

In England, there have been several cases of Teacher-Student relationship and even the couple ending up in love and married! Others have ran away to be together in the midst of charged emotions and feelings. Though it is a wholly inappropriate situation, such relationship require understanding of all concerned and best dealt in private and in counselling with all parties.

Incidentally both the primary and secondary school I attended back home were started by a group of Christian missionaries from Scotland. Bless their good hearts.

English, Mathematics, History and Geography were core subjects taught in the schools and we had to learn at least two other languages beside English. We had the best English Teachers - one, Mr. Fernandez would strike our ears with rubber bands, if we had bad spelling mistakes!

The Headmaster was a rather tall, slim and towering Scotsman, Mr. McGregor - Oh how I remembered being caned by him. Oouch! It was painful but memorable! He always walks about the school ground and corridor carrying the distinguished cane.

Discipline was his middle name and I was caned at least twice after school assembly for having my hair too long. Mr. McGregor instilled the fear of God into us!

There would be total silence, when he walks by. That's the power of the Mac! Mac means 'son of' in Scottish.

Me and my bicycle that got wrecked on school sports day that led to my first date with my school Teacher, Ms Judy.

Mao Tse Tung & China 4 Aspirations

During Chairman Mao Tse Tung's Rule 1949-1976
Chinese aspire to own 4 Things that went round:
Bicycle, Sewing Machine, Fan & Watch.

Feeling Good Riding A Bicycle :

Eco-friendly, zero emissions
Whizzes past traffic jam
No fuel to put in to go
Good for exercise
Strengthen your legs
Carries your shopping
It is not noisy
Feel the wind in your face
Put a smile on your face!
Free Parking especially in the City

Touchdown London

As the brand new Singapore Airlines plane began its descent to land at London Heathrow Airport, gently cutting through floppy cotton clouds, I soon caught a glimpse of rows of houses with chimneys, a few with smoke billowing out.

It was like a scene from the Movie, Mary Poppins, starring one of my favourite English actress Julie Andrews. Looking at the neat row of rooftops, I was wishing for the delicious Mary Poppins to suddenly appear and sail across graciously, with a little help from her airborne umbrella. Supercalifragilisticexpialidocious!

Wonderful stuff and so very magical.

Growing up in the Far East, I was fascinated with all things and everything that was English. From the English Language, Her Majesty the Queen, past Kings & Queens of England and Great Britain's glorious history-very colourful history indeed.

There is a growing number of English educated people in the Far East like myself, and indeed all over the world who are interested and curious about the life of Henry the Eight, Shakespeare, the vast rolling hills of the South of England, charming farms, the very healthy looking English looking black & white cows, the sheep in the meadow, and the green lovely countryside, the BBC, the historic Castles, the bright Red Letter Box (150 post boxes erected during the uncrowned reign of Edward VIII) and the iconic Routemaster or more commonly known as the Red London Buses (first used in 1906),the unmistakable tasty British Marmite, the familiar looking London Black Cab(cir.1937) Mars Bar, and the vibrant pop music scene, all the different accents especially cockney, fish and chips and many colourful aspects and shades of the city of London.

Most of the memorable movies and shows on TV back home in Malaysia & Singapore were British productions, notably James Bond, Chitty Chitty Bang Bang, The Sound of Music, My Fair Lady and Oliver.

All my personal favourites. The British do know how to make

good movies and musicals. They are truly and literally a world class standard of their own. Britain's best export! Britain's sure got talent!

After clearing Immigration, there appeared a figure that I have seen in countless books in primary school. No, not Robin Hood but the very English Bobby!

He looks like he has just come out of the comic and story books we read in school. It was surreal!

London's Calling

As I boarded the Coach that was about to take me into the heart of London, my mind raced back to all the images I have seen of London in books and films. Soon I will be walking the fabled streets of London and taking in all the famous landmarks. There were many nationalities on board – a true testament to London's great fusion and a melting pot of foreigners from all corners and parts of the Globe. Someone once remarked whilst I was visiting Rome. 'In Rome, you can always tell who are the locals and who are the visitors to Rome. Each time the local bus passed the Colosseum, it's the foreigners who will turn their heads.' So it's quite easy to spot the odd foreigners on such an occasion.

An hour later, I just couldn't contain my happiness and excitement and I began to let out a silent scream within, 'Wow to be in London!' as the driver drove past the most famous building in the world.

The very majestic and the very glorious building-Buckingham Palace with the palace horse guards unfolded before my brown eyes as we drove past towards the City Victoria Coach station. It was such a fantastic sight!

So good to see it in real life rather than in books and films. The countless and steady stream of tourists of all nationalities and from all over the world is a grand testament of the popularity of the British Royal Family and Institution.

As I had only eleven hours in the City before I next catch the coach up north to Manchester, I had a list of must see places in London, for that day.

Purchasing a day travel ticket, I soon went on a 'fast track' 'fast speedy Gonzales' tourist 11 hour express deadline mini tour, of the great City of London. Clutching a London underground tube map (first design by Harry Beck in 1931) camera round my neck (yes.... I do really look like the typical Japanese tourist ....click here, click there, click everywhere) I am in a hurry to catch all the sights before I catch the coach at midnight to go up north of England.

London has so much to offer visitors.

It's midday and there I was, all by myself, on British soil watching all things British go by.

Oh to be in London -what a wonderful sight! ... the Red Double Decker bus, so famous all over the world... the Black London Cab ... the Red telephone box, The Tower of London, the historic House of Parliament, The River Thames, Trafalgar Square, Piccadilly Circus, the many Museums, the Beatles Abbey Road, Shopping in Oxford Road, the Hyde Park, No.10 Downing Street ... the colour coded London Underground Network, the Theatres, Big Ben etc etc etc.

Walking through the narrow streets of Covent Garden, I see people sitting in cafes sipping the all- important cup of English tea with scones topped with cream and the lovely parks, and was lucky to catch a glimpse of a group of cockney speaking pearly Kings and Queens.

These iconic images are synonymous with all things British together with grand Buckingham Palace and the changing of the guards, the British queue, and of course not forgetting ... yes the English love of dogs, cats and tea. Not in that order of preference but it's all very English, very British.

Using the London Underground is not as daunting or complicating as it looks. The various station routes are all colour coded, to make it easier for all travellers.

As night fall, I began to make my way to Victoria Coach Station to take the Coach to the North of England.

Few quick facts on London

- People have lived in London for more than 5000 years. Used to be forests and marshes.
- Legend has it that London was founded not by Romans of the 1st century AD, but in ancient time by Brutus the Trojan, around 1070BC.
- London is made up of two ancient cities
  - The City - Financial & Business.
  - The City of Westminster – Parliament & Seat of Government & Buckingham Palace.
- London biggest city in Britain & Europe. *Occupies 620 square miles*
- Population 8.3million. *(2013 census)*
- First City in the world to have underground railway. *(The Tube built in 1863.)*
- Over 100 theatres - 50 are in West End.
- London hosted Olympics games three times.
- Tower Bridge built 1894.
- Tallest Building 2013 - The Shard at 87 stories.
- Tower of London-Built 1080 by William the Conqueror.

Up North of England

The ride up North of England past midnight was indeed long and winding, as we passed through small quaint sleepy villages and towns.

An Englishman once told me in Singapore and these are his actual words. 'If you go pass Watford, a town just outside of London, you would have left England' I am still trying to figure out what he meant. It is a North – South divide issue, historically speaking. Before I arrive in England, I did some research on the North of England.

Many famous cities are located up North of England. Birmingham (the locals pronounced it as BirminGUM,) Leeds & Manchester – home of Manchester United and the iconic building, Old Trafford.

Accents & Dialects –Tuning in with your Eastern Ears!

Northern English is one of the major groupings of English dialects. The others being East Anglian English, East and the and West Midlands English, West Country (Somerset, Devon, Cornwall) and Southern English.

For people from the Far East it may take some time for your ears to pick up and appreciate the different regional accents. The Northern dialects includes the Yorkshire and Lancashire dialects, and that of the North East England and the Cumbria region.

Historically, the North East of England County has a Viking influence but the Norwegian has a greater impact on most Northern dialects.

It will be difficult at first to make out what the natives say, but after sometime it will be clearer, if you pick out the main words from their speech.

Having lived and worked with them over the years, I am still struggling to understand some words and vice versa.

So do ask them to repeat, if you are not so sure, what is coming out from their mouths. They will understand most foreigners do have difficulty – even their own English natives face problems understanding each other!

Northern English contains the following dialects:

- » Mancunian, which is spoken in Greater Manchester and some parts of Lancashire and eastern Cheshire.
- » Yorkshire dialects and accents in Yorkshire.
- » Teeside dialects /accents spoken in Middlesbrough and surrounding areas.
- » Cumbrian dialect in Lake District areas.
- » Geordie spoken in the Newcastle/Tyneside area which include Northumberland and parts of County Durham.
- » Lancashire accents.
- » Mackem in Sunderland/Wearside.
- » Pitmatic in mining community in County Durham and Northumberland.
- » Scouse is spoken in Liverpool where the Beatles come from. It is also spoken in Merseyside of Liverpool, in parts of west Cheshire and along the North Wales coast.

To hear the different accents, go online to check on Youtube and you will get an idea of the tone and the pronunciations. Other fascinating accents can be found in the Scottish, Irish and the London Cockney accents.

There are various interesting video clips.

Having travelled more than eighteen hours including the stopover in London, I just could not help but envy all the people behind closed doors fast asleep in their warm comfortable beds as the coach needled its way through the sleepy terrace houses.

At Birmingham, a group of passenger including an elderly lady in her sixties and her two relatives got on board. Apparently they have all just got back from a holiday in Spain. How did I know? Well they sat next to me and from their conversation had flights delayed and were sure glad to be heading home to Manchester.

It seems to me, the majority of the British do appreciate the good life and work, save and splash on a good holiday abroad. Back home, the majority of parents tend to work and save for their children. I can still remember my father's friend and grocer. The very good and workaholic, Mr. Wang.

A Very Workaholic Wang

When I was a boy of ten, my father used to take me to his grocery shop to buy provisions. Mr Wang would always be sitting behind the cash counter, wearing a white T-shirt and brown shorts and his right arm resting on a unique Chinese calculator, the abacus ever ready to calculate and receive payments from customers.

Ten years later, I walked into the shop and couldn't believe my eyes! There he was – Mr. Wang sitting behind the cash register, in white T-shirt and brown shorts and his right hand resting on the abacus.

Gosh, it was as if time stood still, and from his facial expression he does looked like he was being glued quite permanently to his seat and never moved all these years! I felt like screaming at him, to go out and enjoy himself instead of still voluntarily being stuck in the shop all these years, slogging away, day in and day out.

Mr. Wang came from the old school, his grandfather like mine came from China.

Seeing Mr. Wang slogging away and remembering how tough life were for him and my forefathers, I felt like telling him 'Hey Uncle, chill out, take a break, you do deserve it, after all these years!'

It is so sad to think the poor hardworking chap sweats away in the shop while his two sons are lapping it up in Europe. All I can say is Mr. Wang is a caring father who works hard for his sons and family.

Some people would say Mr. Wang is a bit foolish for working so very hard, but not enjoying the fruits of his labour. The older generation do not put holiday on the top of their leisure list, in those days.

The troubled times and harsh life they experienced in old China constantly remind them to be frugal and focus on being productive.

Their minds are preoccupied with feeding themselves with three square meals a day. If the English think Mr. Wang's name is unusual or funny, wait till you meet my schoolmate, by the name of Ting Tong Pong! Last I heard, he was working for an alarm system company. If you google his name it will show up in Facebook.

Foggy & Wet Manchester.

It's 4 am in the morning of a freezing cold December.

The streets in the city of Manchester is hauntingly peaceful and quiet with a handful of people walking by, as I got off the coach in Manchester Piccadilly Coach Station, in the heart of the city.

As arranged earlier, my hometown friend Chow, who is a Teacher by profession and who has lived in England for over ten years would be picking me up from the station.

Only the changing of colours of the traffic lights kept me entertained, while waiting for my friend to pick me up. It's bitterly cold but the surrounding new and old buildings and the lovely gardens do look welcoming. Right on time, I was picked up and with the comforting warm air blowing around the car, we headed to Chow's flat in a place called Cheetham Hill – just on the outskirt of Manchester City.

It was such a great relief soon after to be able to lie down in a warm bed and stretched my weary legs and tired body. As my dizzy dozzy head pressed against the soft comfy pillows, I could just about, almost hear Paul McCartney's velvet voice rendering the smooth 'the long and winding road that leads to your door … don't leave me waiting here … '

England, here I am lying in a bed on your British soil and can't wait till daybreak to see and experience local life.

It has taken a long life dream started in primary school to be finally to be in England.

A Drive by Historic & Cosmopolitan Manchester.

As dawn broke and after breakfast, Chow took me out on a sight-seeing and historical drive around the City and the surrounding areas.

I had the pleasure of trying a full English Big Breakfast consisting of bacon, eggs, sausages, mushrooms, beans and some crusty toast finished with a lovely cup of English Typhoo tea. Brilliant!

Over breakfast Chow mentioned that Manchester can boast of some very prominent people - the Movers and Shakers as we know them in modern society today.

Men and Women who brought change to society and left lasting legacy. It is worth noting the city has more Noble Peace Prize Holders nationally.

'Let me take you on a quick tour of the city of Manchester with a bit of history afterwards' Chow kindly offered the invitation, after gulping down the last drop of his tea.

As we drove down the main road of the village of Cheetham Hill, the morning burst to life with mainly dark skin people walking by and shops displaying and selling all kinds of everything.

'Where have all the English gone?' I asked Chow.

'Ah, this is largely an immigrant area, where some of the 27,200 Asians mainly Gujaratis of Indian origin holding British passports expelled from Idi Amin Uganda, came in 1972' he replied. Chow is a teacher of statistics by profession and he knows his numbers. He chews numbers and facts for breakfast!

'See the five storey buildings there' Chow pointed out as we drove past the half completed structure. 'They will be named after the British women's rights activist Emmerline Pankhurst, who led the British suffragette movement to win the right for women to vote.'

Moving ahead we drive to the Prestwich - Whitefield suburbs where there is a large Jewish Community.

They came to set up homes in Manchester after escaping Nazi Germany in 1942. Even though Jews have been living in Britain since the Norman Conquest of 1066 or even earlier.

They came as merchants and money lenders because the Christian faith of their ruling masters forbid loans with interest - Jews are considered tight with their money, as historically they were money lenders.

Many today are firmly part of the middle class in professional or highly skilled jobs in England.

The Scottish people are also known to be quite tight with their money like the Jews according to some.

'The Jews have been living in Britain for over 200 years and is the second largest community at over 280, 000 in UK' remarked Chow.

The Jews have been persecuted for most of their lives –being made scapegoats when times are bad by their host country. They were first expelled from England in 1290, as decreed by King Edward I, and years later readmitted in 1656.Unlike the Middle Ages where they were persecuted and put in Ghettos, to separate them from the locals all over Europe, the Jews have perservered and they have prospered in business and the professions.

Benjamin Disraeli a Jew by birth became Prime Minister of Great Britain in 1868.Yehudi Menuhin, Amy Winehouse, Peter Sellers and Lord Alan Sugar are all great examples of the British Jews success story.

Making a U turn we then head towards the venue of the Commonwealth Games held in the city in 2002. The Games provided the catalyst for the transformation of Manchester and created new jobs and opportunities.

Chow said that the Games brought a new spirit and hope to the City after years of uncertainty.

Chow in his Chinese humour then asked if I had enjoyed the Napoli Italian ice cream we had in Napoli a year ago, mimicking the Italian accent.

'Bella, bella, molto bene . . . eh . . . mama mia'

We are in Ancoats nestled just on the fringe of the City. This is the Napoli of Manchester - A Little Italy.

The earliest Italians who came in the 1800 were a floating population of peddlers and street musicians.

More working class folks came and found homes in the slums

of Ancoats - some making a living starting out as ice cream vendors and barrel organists.

I love all things Italian - the pasta, wine and music and Italy is my favourite holiday destination. Whenever I meet any anglicised Italians in England, I always ask them to say a few Italian phrases and tell them not to forget their roots and be Italiano, when they start to speak and sound like the local native, Mancunian.

It is always good to remember where one comes from and to be just yourself, true to your own original ethnic identity and culture, but being respectful of others in the community.

Chow next insisted I should see the many fine surviving warehouses –many being resurrected under the city regeneration building programme.

Chow related to me the scenario of the late 18thand 19th Century. How during the period of the Industrial Revolution, Manchester was the hub of a network of smaller towns. Lancashire towns and hence dominated the production of cotton goods nationally and internationally. It was nicknamed 'Cottonopolis.' The other industries were the chemical production, precision engineering and above all freight.

We saw the Royal Exchange Theatre and The Corn Exchange Shopping Centre which used to house the main trading floors for cotton and corn, respectively. These buildings of a glorious age have recently been renovated and converted into living apartments.

Another massive brick rectangle building now a leisure complex was once the docking and transfer point which was linked to the city's road, rail and canal networks.

Looking at these buildings I could just about imagine how busy it must be in those days, with all the noise and movements of goods and people - behind those drawn curtains of the now ornate buildings.

Of course we cannot cover all the history of Manchester in a couple of hours in our mini tour but Chow thought a trip to see the Bridgewater canal and the Manchester Ship Canal opened in 1894 was not to be missed given the important role the play in the economic growth of the Region

Chow urged me to imagine ocean-going ships that were navigating the 58 kilometres stretch all the way from Liverpool to Port of Manchester located in nearby Salford and Trafford. The port no longer exist and in its place stand postmodern high-rise buildings and apartments with retail facilities, museum and the concert halls around the docking areas.

At the time of the visit with Chow the new BBC HQ Media City building project was still in its planning stage but I did noticed some ground levelling work at that site. On the way back we passed the world famous stadium - Manchester United Football Stadium and also had a view of the Old Trafford grounds. The various faculties of the University Manchester next came into view as Chow drove along Oxford Road to show me the Centres of Learning and the university buildings all around the campus. Chow pointed out the Royal Northern College of Music. 'This College is world class and has students from all over the globe' and proudly so for Chow as he has a sister studying violin there.

Manchester is a popular destination and choice of further and university tertiary studies for overseas students from as far as the Far East.

Manchester Aloud!

The City has a strong historical link with the University and education. The region is now an economic knowledgeled centre. The university research has been ranked as the third most powerful in the UK behind Oxford and Cambridge, in terms of research.

Mention the name of Manchester, and a number of image spring to mind. Football and rain are two of them.

The City is credited with giving the world the Industrial Revolution of the 18th century.

A boom in the textile manufacturing business during the Industrial Revolution, resulted in it becoming the world's first Industrialised City

Manchester was the site of the world's first passenger railway station and many scientific achievements of great importance.

In the Roman period it was known as 'Mamucium' built as a

wooden fort in 80AD by General Julius Agicola, protecting a Roman road from the ruling Celtic tribe of the North West. Manchester had a very humble origin. Romans are renowned for building straight roads. The arrival of Flemish weavers and cloth makers in the 14th century, marked the start ofManchester as a major player in the textile industry.

The Green Green Grass of Home? (well, almost!)

Chow then drove us on to our last stop in the history tour. An area we both can identify within our custom and culture. Yes, we parked the car and took a stroll down Chinatown.

'You know' I said to Chow 'There are Chinatowns in almost every cities in the world, even in the artic!'

'Ya' Chow concurred.

While walking down Chinatown in a foreign land, I felt a sense of Chineseness (if ever there was such a word).I felt a closeness to my kinsmen and to my traditions and culture as most Chinese all over the world feel when they meet another Chinese in a foreign land.

There is a kind of reassurance and safety and connection when we speak to each other in our dialect –be it Hokkien, Teo Chew, Hakka, Kek, or the Cantonese as is more widely spoken among the Hong Kong Chinese in Manchester. A lot of walls are broken down when we speak to one another in our own dialects. I tried this once in a Restaurant when it was almost closing time for a lunch buffet and the Boss very kindly extended the time, to allow me and a friend to have our lunch.

Have you eaten?

To the Chinese eating well is a sign of prosperity and that is why family love gathering around a table for a meal with lots of dishes, as one would observe in a Chinese Restaurant.

Among the very first greetings exchanged when two Oriental

persons meet are, 'How are you and have you eaten? This is almost universal in nature whilst the British will talk about the weather.

Chinese New Year is our Christmas!

As we approached the Grand Arch in Chinatown, Chow mentioned that it is here that the yearly Chinese New Year Celebrations take place. To us it is the most important day, like Christmas to the British. Standing under the impressive Arch, memories of my first celebration of this auspicious day started flowing back.

On eve of Chinese New Year we have the compulsory family dinner, where tradition dictate all members of the family should come home for family reunion dinner.

Hence all the Chinese in China and elsewhere drop everything to head home for this gathering. A sign of respect for the parents, elders and family members.

There will be no sweeping of the floors on the eve of the big day - as good luck will be swept away and my parents will dress us in new clothes, ready to bring in the New Lunar Year.

Kung Hee Fatt Choy!

On the Chinese New Year day itself, all the Children will look forward to receiving the traditional Red packet or Ang Pow, which contain money in it.

This is given by married couples and Parents to their children and other kids of family and the unmarried. A sign of giving for prosperity and good luck to come.

The British gives presents and we give the Red Packets known as Ang Pows. Can't be more different than this! Ang means red and pow is the packet.

The celebrations usually have a dragon dance display in public in Chinatowns and worldwide and end with the sound of spectacular fire crackers to drive off evil and bad spirit. We celebrate for fifteen days and hours of eating and merrymaking.

Many English people have asked me how come the Chinese are so slim despite eating a lot! It's the rice!

Eating Stalls and places in the Far East from Beijing, Hong Kong, Taiwan, Hong Kong to Singapore are open very long hours some till past midnight.

Manchester City has benefitted with the influx of a host of foreign and exotic menus as is evidenced in the Chinatown and surrounding areas where there is a good mix of international restaurants.

We ended the tour with a bowl of Cantonese wanton - a traditional dish of prawns and noodles sprinkled with some fine pak choy vegetables and downed with a lovely hot Chinese jasmine tea.

Wah! Just dumplingly delicious!

The Chinese are one of the largest ethnic minority in the City, third largest Chinese population after London and South East and make up 2.7% of the 2.68million population according to census 2013. The majority are in the food and catering industry, restaurants, takeaways and others in the various businesses and enterprises and many of the new generation in managerial and professional occupations. The first wave of Chinese arrivals to the city were from Tianjin and Shanghai in the early 19th century and settled in port cities like Liverpool.

Beside the availability of different varieties, there are many diverse plates of different ethnic dishes.

It has been a wonderful tour and a brief walk down history of Manchester, and as I thank Chow for taking time to show me round, he offered to show me more of the off beaten track next time.

Goodness Gracious, the Curry is Delicious!

That evening he took me to Rusholme or more commonly known to locals as the Curry Mile of Manchester. Rows of brightly lit shops selling all kinds of everything and Indian Restaurants greeted us even at 11pm. The streets and lights were dazzling, just like back home, where shops never seem to close. As we were walking to the Restaurant for our evening meal, Chow pointed out that the BBC pop show 'Top of the Pops' had a studio here and it was here in

1964 that the Rolling Stones and the Manchester bred, The Hollies recorded a live studio show in the bohemian and swinging sixties.

The Curry Mile lived up to its name as the meal was very authentic and excellent value for money.

The Indian Entrepreneurs who set up the business here have brought a new kind of exotic dishes and tastes to the British public, who are now more eager to try new cuisines from around the world, partly due to travels abroad and some good food TV shows. Ah Ghanji, very good curry . . . it feels just like home.

Manchester On the Move!

Since hosting the 2002 Commonwealth Games in Manchester, the City itself has been transformed and has regenerated itself from a post war Industrial hub to a modern cosmopolitan vibrant city.

It can boast of having 25 Nobel prize - winners more than all but seven nations and a home of creativity. Other first for the city include the Anti-Corn League a model for later political lobbying group, the Green, the many firsts in Science, Engineering, Medical, Transport, the Arts

Computing, and especially in the field of aviation.

In 1830 the world's true railway line began from a purpose built rail station on Liverpool Road. The first Marks and Spencer store opened in Manchester in 1894. Alan Turing, Manchester computer pioneer add a first too with his breaking of the Enigma code.

Other badges of honour for Manchester include the setting up of the first municipal airport in the United Kingdom in 1929.Former Manchester Central High School students. J W Alcock and A W Brown, were the first to fly the Atlantic Ocean non-stop in 1919.

Local Mancunian, AV Roe, designed and flew the first all British aeroplane in 1908.He also pioneered the enclosed plane cockpit and the joystick. His Avro Avians, made became the first aeroplane to complete a solo flight to Australia, putting another feather in the First Manchester Cap. There is even a UFO landing airport – some kind of landing strip in the New Hulme area of Manchester!

Today in the year 2014, the Architecture landscape of the City has been transformed and it has an 'upbeat and feeling good' factor.

Even brown land and old industrial sites have been brought to life in the form of modern and stylish apartment. Thanks to visionary property developer like Tom Bloxham of Urban Splash.

Driving away from the bright lights of the city and going past all the new modern buildings blending in with the old Victorian buildings, Chow informed me that the people of Manchester do have a spirit like the slogan in Nike 'Just Do It !' instead of talking about it.

Look who is famous and from Manchester

- » Sir Joseph Whitworth—Industrialist and pioneer of precision engineering.
- » Roy Chadwick—designer of the Lancaster bomber.
- » Ernest Rutherford—first person to split the atom.
- » Sir Bernard Lovell—creator of the giant radio—telescope at Jodrell Bank and pioneer of radio astronomy.
- » Sir Alan Turing—founder of computer science. He was credited with cracking the German code with Enigma.
- » Maurice, Barry & Robin Gibb—The Bee Gees first started out in Chorlton.
- » Davy Jones of The Monkees
- » Peter Noone of The Herman Hermits
- » Graham Nash of Crosby, Stills, Nash & Young.
- » Rick Astley pop singer.
- » Russell Watson   Classical singer from Irlam.
- » World famous Architect, Norman Foster.
- » David Lloyd George   British Prime Minister.
- » Emmeline Pankhurst, suffragette leader. Led campaign for the right of women to vote.
- » Ricky Hatton—Boxer.
- » Paul Scholes—Footballer.
- » Manchester United Football Team.

Oh To Be in England!

On my very first day in a very cold England, I noticed the shopkeepers and majority of the native English people in general are all very civilized, and generally people are polite. Lots of thank you and please. A Culture Shock!

Someone once said England was the land of milk and honey. From observation there are plenty of cows and roaming around the English' rolling hills. I am still in search of the gold honey pot. They also say the streets of London are paved with gold. But from what I have seen since I arrived, some streets are paved more with chewing gum! A very ugly sight of England indeed.

In Singapore the import of chewing gum is banned and one can be issued with a hefty fine. In the opinion of the Government the chewing gum is a nuisance in public and an eye sore. Fines range from US$500 to a jail term. There have been instances of the sticky chewing gum jamming the doors of trains, & defacing of few prestigious buildings and places.

No, it is not a pretty sight at all and not eco-friendly, at all. In quite a number of towns and cities in England, one is greeted by the unique 'Gummy Walk of Fame' which do appear like decorations in the town pavements and streets. Councils throughout England have a very tough and difficult task of removing this sticky stuff and it is a costly exercise and so unnecessary.

In Singapore you will be fined and charged for littering. In 1992 the import and the chewing of gum was banned. In Singapore. Fines vary from US500-US1000 for first time offenders.

There are also fines for many types of littering, spitting, defacing property, jaywalking and vandalizing in the city. American Student, Michael Fay was caned and jailed for vandalizing cars in 1994. It is fine here, fine there! The joke floating is, Singapore is a Fine City.

Ang Mo – The English

In British ruled Singapore and Malaya, 'Ang Mo' was a colloquial term for a Caucasian person and it has been used till this day to refer to the White English. Ang in Chinese Hokkien dialect means Red and Mo is hair-literally translate as 'red hair'

From my personal observation living in England, I would offer to say the English are generally polite and courteous and they are conditioned from an early age, at home and in school to say the two very important words, that stay with them for the rest of their lives. The two golden words are 'Thank You' and 'Please'. Foreigners in England will do well, and go far, to note them and use these essential words daily.

These two words are sadly not as well used in the Far East especially in China, Hong Kong, Singapore and other neighbouring countries. People there feel that they are already paying for all services required and therefore can't see why they have to say thank you - their focus is money.

Average British says 5,000 Thank You per year!

According to a newspaper survey in mid-2000, the average British would have said 'thank you' 5,000 times a year, fourteen times a day, a third throw in a cheers or ta, one in twenty interviewed are keen on nice one and the younger generation opt for cool, 70% of those surveyed confessed they will sometime say the words without meaning it.

In contrast the average Chinese in China would only say 'thank you' three times a day. Britain is such a polite society; sometimes it does seem the amount of 'thank-you' (on average five from my observation for each transaction) said by an individual paying at the till of the supermarket and petrol station may have contributed to the queue.

In Hong Kong, they would have grab the money off your hands before you could even say 'excuse me' or 'Bob is your uncle' and you'd be lucky to get a thank you or smile in return.

Embedded in the British psyche is their sense of fair play and their tendency to side with the weaker underdog but they can be quite sceptical, if you come across as being too forthright. At other times they can be seen as too lenient or leaning too much on the idea of liberalism and the rights of the individual at the expense of others.

For example, squatters seem to have more rights than the owner of the home property they are occupying. Funny law? Their sense of fair play may sometimes bend on the path of being seen as polite in war against the enemy - the British are very conscious of the fact they should treat their enemies in a fair but firm manner. One thing I have noticed is that the English do not smile unless they have a good reason, unlike me and people from the Far East. I once heard an English man said that he need to read the daily papers so he won't be seen as being too happy, otherwise people will think he is high on drugs! Gosh! This was news to me! No wonder the English think I may be high on something! The Chinese do smile when they are embarrassed.

The Inventive and D. I. Y English

Quite a large majority of English are D. I. Y. Enthusiasts. Back home even changing a light bulb was a big event when I was growing up.

My parents will phone for the Electrician and my brothers and I will stand well back and watched in amazement as he skilfully replace a bulb, without getting electrocuted. We were terrified of touching the bulb, even when the electricity is switched off!

As kids were often cautioned about the danger of electricity, but since coming to England, I have found out it is actually quite safe to change a bulb on your own! Cost of labour is cheap back then and health and safety information was limited or non-existing.

Sometimes I think the bad cold weather in England in winter

keep the Natives in, and that's when they become creative thinkers. It is worth noting that the English or the larger society, the British have been at the forefront of inventions and discoveries - in so many fields.

The Gentle Englishmen

When I read about British Soldiers facing tribunals about mistreating their enemies, I sometime want to shout out loud 'For Goodness sake, you are at war and not at a friendly paint ball shooting game in your local park!'

Even shouting at the enemy to get answers can be seen as harsh? I wondered if this could be due to a sense of guilt of British's empirical past (where the sun never sets in the far east) raiding foreign countries and the Commonwealth of their enormous wealth.

At times it seem the English are afraid to correct certain issues created by the minorities of other faiths, for fear of being accused of racism. But this attitude is slowly changing, now in 2014.

The British Empire Builders

To be fair to the empire builders, British rule in countries such as Singapore and Malaya brought lots of benefits and developments in terms of education, law and order, and political stability.

On a personal level, my own grandparents were brought by a British merchant ship to Singapore, after escaping from the civil war and troubles during the conflict of the warlords in China. I have indeed a lot to be grateful to the British for helping those in times of need and dire circumstances, whilst rightly or wrongly helping themselves to the fortunes of their newly discovered gems and territories in the East, the Nanyang, as the adventurers new emigrants Chinese call it.

It's Bonkers! Flipping Heck! Cor Blimey!

Another aspect that I found quite fascinating is the different accents and the use of words and sentences throughout the British Isle from Scotland to London. The accents are so different and distinguished, and in many ways, funny and strange to an eastern ear.

When I first arrived in London, I was greeted by a lovely looking lady at the airport 'how nice of you to come to England' after chatting her up, and months later, visiting Liverpool I was greeted with 'eee what the bloody hell are you doing here lad?' by a Liverpool man.

In Bradford, I was greeted by a gentleman by these warm and welcoming words 'Welcome to Bradford, so when are you going back?' Cor blimey, the British are a friendly lot; they don't like to take themselves too seriously and do have a good sense of humour.

The British Class System

A legacy and feature of colonial Britain which is less obvious and dominant today but still evident in the education system and social life of the nation - is very much part of the make-up of the society.

Different classes of people here read different newspapers and publications and mixed in different social groups according to their level of education and background. They also communicate differently.

It was amusing to learn that the upper classes call their Fathers, Papa. Back home and most Chinese around the globe used this term of endearment when we call ours, regardless of class. A bin man back home would call his dad, Papa. Majority of English call their father, Dad. It will sound like Darth to our ears.

In the past, their social background - this included family status, class, accent, to some extent determine their career opportunities. A British Comedian joked that in the past, having a Geordie accent can be seen and considered to be so detrimental to one's life that one can be considered for disability allowance! He was referring to people from Newcastle, the North East England area.

Today with education, social mobility and new avenue of opportunities, this trend is slowly changing.

According to news report in 2006, there are now seven different classes in Britain.

The Elite make up 6%, Established middle class 25%, Technical middle class 6%, new affluent worker 15%, Traditional working class 14%, Emergent service worker 19% and the Precariat 15% - these are the most deprived and the poorest group in Society.

They score low in educational, social and cultural factors and tend to mix in their own social grouping.

Quite a number of the musicians I have met seem to come from this working class group in England.

It is such a wonderful feeling to see so many of them using their talent, to overcome adversity.

Music can provide a way out of poverty and bring some measure of wealth and success to them.

I got to know a few on a more on a personal level and hear their tales of joy and sadness, as they struggle to make a living as a busker and then progressing to work for my artiste agency, earning £130 per performance.

It is a heart-warming story, as I have got to know a few of them on a more personal friendship level.

The British DNA

The Lonely Planet, Great Britain, 8th Edition had this to say about the British.

"Calmness in the face of adversity, a laconic sense of humour, a sense of decency and fair play, and mastery of understatement" are all fundamental facets of the British Character-at least, as seen by the British themselves.

Ask the French and you might get a rather different list of attributes that include stand-offishness, anti-intellectualism, public drunkenness and being crap at cooking."

"The nostalgic English —especially after a few pints can get downright weepy about their white cliffs of Dover." - Frommer's England 2010 (source: Internet)

The English sacred Queue

Another distinguished feature of British culture is their orderly queue for things.

Be it for park rides, buses, train tickets or to pay at the counter, queuing is sacrosanct and woe betide anyone who get this wrong. Few things are more calculated to spark an outburst of tutting about as publicly cross as most Brits get-than 'pushing in' at a queue.

The English & New Opportunities

The music business is one of the few industries left, like football, where education does not dictate success or failure. Your talent and passion for and love of music and musical instinct plays the biggest part in your success.

Once I was reading the Financial Times during a break in a part-time job at a well - established bakery. I could see the astonishment from the looks of my co-workers and one of them even asked me in plain English 'Can you read?' and 'Oh, have you gone all posh reading this pinky paper?' I suspect he couldn't believe a factory worker, let alone a foreigner, could digest its contents.

To me, the class system is a reflection of a divided society where different classes of people are slotted in different pigeon-holes with different expectations of hope and aspiration. When I was growing up, back home in Singapore and Malaysia, the majority of children have equal access to good quality teaching and we all read almost similar newspapers and mixed with all pupils from all classes of the society. The rich and the poor.

In the UK there seem to be an unequal access to good quality facilities and Teachers for some. The fee paying private and public school pupils appear to have a better life chance than those poorer pupils from state schools.

According to an article in The Independent by Mark Steel, Class still rules. It is just the jobs that have changed. 77% Judges and 55% Senior Company Directors are Oxford and Cambridge educated and in 2010 almost 45% of the pupils in these two prestigious universities were from the public schools.

What defined class is today more complex. Mining work and other traditional working class jobs have been replaced in call centres, which employ three times more staff than the docks and mining industry in its hey days. Tesco employs over 250, 000 workers and can rival that of a big ship building firm and other disbanded industries and workshops.

Today with a changing multi-cultural pattern and the economy, a new Britain is evolving and it is slowly eroding the one time class – ridden society. Still, some features of the British class system continue to exist- accents, clothes, interests, education and type of food.

British Comedian Simon Evans joked that working class Britons can ever be so proud of their very own exclusivity. 'To join the Matalan Store, one has to be a member - and if you have a quid and know where you live, you are in' I love his very English sense of humour!

Working with the English Natives – I am a Baker!

During the long winter Christmas holidays, I thought it would be an excellent idea to get to know the local English natives and see how they actually think, live and work, by getting a labouring job in a local Bread factory.

The Warburtons Bakery in the North West is a family business and was established in 1876 by a chap named Thomas Warburton.

Based in Bolton, Lancashire, it has a workforce of well over 5,000 and its brand name is ahead of Cadburys and Walkers Crips.

After a successful interview at the recruitment agency based about ten-minute walk from the Bakery, the Consultant, a blonde lady, took us to meet the Manager of the Company.

As we were walking there she somehow lost the direction and in a flash, I suggested we follow the smell of bread that we were sensing along the way. Eventually our nose led us right to the door of the factory.

After an initial briefing, we were shown round the factory floors of the different sections - the mixing room, the production line, the huge oven, the packing and loading and the rest room, canteen, toilets and changing rooms.

Reporting for work the following week on a night shift working from 6pm- 6am, along twelve hour rota, I was sent to the production line.

Pure & Simple from Baker Street

The job was very pure and simple. All I had to do is to put the bite size dough of flour that was coming towards me, into a baking can.

It was relatively easy but can get boring. So I passed the time thinking of certain mathematical problems or trying to remember lyrics to songs or things or issues I have to sort out.

About five weeks into the job, I was transferred to the oven section. It was in the middle of a very cold winter.

I loved it - it was just like the tropical heat back in Singapore. Warm and cosy and there was the bonus of getting a free sun tan!

There were two of us at this operation and we were told never to leave our position.

As the baked products come out from the oven, we were to take the trays with our heavily padded gloves and bang it on these wooden logs to dislodge the breads on to the conveyor belt that leads to another section. The empty trays are then slotted in a standing rack.

One night the Jamaican guy, Steve who was my partner excused himself to go to the toilet.

'Only two or three minutes, ya man, OK? ' he asked.

'Ya man, I am OK, brother' I responded with some hesitation, hoping he won't be too long.

'Cool Brother' Steve, my newly discovered Jamaican brother said, as he walked away, singing a reggae song and swaying his 5ft 6" body from side to side. Give me hope, Joanna, Give me hope, Joanna, Give me hope . . .'

I could see the baked tea cakes in a row of four big trays coming half way - like an armada of army tanks in the distance, in the brightly orange flamed oven.

Each tray measured about 26 inches by 26 inches and hold about 40 tea cakes. There must have been over 100 trays approaching!

Into the Fire!

After three minutes has passed, there was no sign of Steve at all. I was getting a little bit anxious.

The trays were now two minutes to reach the end of the line. I started to look again for Steve.

When there was not a sighting of him after a couple of minutes, I started to look around for someone, anyone who could help, if Steve don't make it back soon.

Not a soul was around.

Looking into the huge oven, I started to worry as I could see the long line of big trays, in four rows coming very near to the end.

It was as if Hitler was sending his troops in their German army tanks to attack me by the hundreds!

Each of us was supposed to bang the trays –two for each worker, on the logs, for the bread to fall onto a conveyor belt that leads to the wrapping section.

As the trays all reached the end of the line, I picked up my two trays and did my part and tried to do the same for Steve. All this while the other trays were back to back, coming forward. The huge Oven was very long and seemed to go on forever. Try as quick and as best that I can on my own, the trays just came smashing into each other, like a big car crash, jack-knifing into each other! It was a disaster zone with what looked like dead bodies of tea cakes all over the floor!

Just then, Steve appeared and seeing the mayhem all around us, he quickly took all the metal trays that was jammed up against each other on the conveyor line and just threw them on the floor.

The alarm bell must have sounded, as the Supervisor was soon running towards us.

'Oh, what the friggin hell is all this shite?' he shouted in disbelief at the sight of the fallen tea cakes all over the floor.

More workers came to help eventually and soon we were back to normal. Steve apologised and said he was not feeling well and had to 'sit it out'.

Steve and I were soon send packing to the packing unit!

If as F and Kick as Cake

Mixing with the locals I have also discovered different areas have their own local phrases and words that they use on a daily basis. It is a struggle for any foreigner to try and understand some of the northern accents.

The Irish Chap working with me in the dough mixing section pronounced six as sex, first as fast, this as des, and If as F, church as churt, bus as bush and kick as cake. I have annoyed him on more than several occasions by not being able to understand what he said and he has not a clue what I was trying to say with my Chinese pronunciation and accent. Partners made in heaven!

I can truly say they treated me well and are the true 'salt of the earth' as the English would say.

Phrases like 'I like 'em me' which I understand it to mean 'I like it' can seem a bit strange if you are not used to it, like I did, where they speak it in certain areas.

Till today, I still do not know or understand why they have put the word 'me' at the end of the phrase. I still find it fascinating to hear the various accents every day in the streets and whilst travelling around Great Britain.

Who ate all the pies?

It was a hilarious time in the bakery especially when they taught me a song 'Who ate all the pies' and asked me to sing it in front of the huge and overweight night supervisor, when he came round to check on work in progress. Like a fool, I sang it out loudly and boldly- as instructed by my three English work colleagues in the packing room, just as the Supervisor came. He looked at me in utter disbelief and luckily he and the other three gentlemen, broke out laughing! I would have got the sack, if not for the humour loving Supervisor. He was a huge guy!

I can truly say they treated me well and are the true 'salt of the earth' as the English would say.

Experiencing British working life with Bakery workers

Phrases like 'I like 'em me' which I understand it to mean 'I like it' can seem a bit strange if you are not used to it, like I did.

Till today, I still do not know or understand why they have put the word 'me' at the end of the phrase. I still find it curious to hear the locals saying 'It's me dad' instead of 'It's my dad' or 'It's me day off' and why they call lunch as dinner and dinner as tea?

Frankly, it is a warm feeling, when you hear it.

Often the mum of my English friends will say 'Come on in love, what's to do? Have a cuppa tea love. '

I find it all very earthy and a feeling of Home away from Home! There is a sense of 'don't worry, we will look after you, lad' kind of feeling in the air.

Generally the Northerners are friendly, down to earth and easy to get along with. The majority of them are polite, honest and possess a sense of fair play.

The Greatness of a Nation and its moral progress can be judged by the way its animals are treated.

Mahatma Gandhi

The Lucky Dogs of England

The British's humanitarian nature can be seen in the ways they treat and care for the animals especially dogs. Some are eccentric hence the tag 'mad dog and Englishmen' has been banded about. The line between creativity and eccentricity is somewhat blurred. Mahatma Gandhi said 'The greatness of a Nation and its moral progress can be judged by the way its animals are treated.' Great Britain can be proud of the love and care they give to their pets.

In the Far East people tend to keep dogs as guard dogs. In some countries, sadly such dogs, cats and other animals are badly and cruelly mistreated. One cannot imagine how inhumane it is to cage an animal in a small confine space, where they cannot even turn around. I am ashamed to say, as a Chinese, some of my own folks in the far Northern China mistreat dogs and in some areas the dog is a delicacy on the dining table!

The tiger and donkey penis are supposed to boost your sexual prowess. How ridiculous and exploitative this money making medicinal claims are!

As a Chinese, I ashamed of my own race for their action.

These cruel evil people who are engaged in this trade are really vile and should be caught and condemned. The terrible gross cruelty to the animals especially those endangered species are done in the name of greed and commerce. Personally I must salute the British for their humanitarian attitudes towards animals.

A painful experience with a dog named Bo!

Personally I love dogs. They are so affectionate and I think girls like them because they don't talk back!

I remember a painful moment when I was a kid of seven.

One morning when I was about to go out for my morning run, I saw my neighbour's dog staring menacingly at me and growling. I was a bit apprehensive and told my elder brother Cheng. He took one quick look at Bo and said 'Don't worry, he is harmless, but if he goes after you, I shall protect you' Feeling assured I ran, Bo ran after me and my protective assuring brother also ran but in the opposite direction into our house, laughing as he did. My protective brother! My foot! Or in this case, my bleeding backside!

Oh gosh who let the dog out? . . . Bo the dog made a meal out of me! It was a painful experience indeed!

What a splendid idea! vs It's mint!

Another distinct feature that I noticed about the British and their way of life is their unique class divisions. Different social classes in the UK read different newspapers, go to different schools, mix in different social circles, holiday and visit different countries and during their vacations, enjoy different recreational activities and uses and speak in different words and phrases.

The stereo type working class gentleman (in the North of England, they are known as blokes) would rise up early 6 30 am in the morning in his council flat, have his toasties and a cup of English tea, reads popular press, The Sun newspaper and head to the factory /his work place and have his dinner (lunch as we call it) at 1pm and return home for his tea (dinner as we call it) after work and at some point in the week , possibly go down to the pub to meet his 'mates' (back home we say friends).

He would most likely enjoy a pint of bitter (a beer –there are many variety here unlike home, where we have only one local – the Tiger Beer) and seek out the latest news on 'me favourite football team'. His traditional love of baked beans, chips and sausages now alternate with the more exotic Indian curry dish and Mediterranean, plus the Chinese fried ups.

His children would normally go to a State school, although this is changing as new opportunities and government initiatives and provisions and higher family income see more from the lower income group attend private education.

The middle class chap wakes up in his semi-detached house to the smell of omelettes and coffee, reads the Daily Mail or The Guardian, drive to work, have his lunch (as they call it) at 1pm and dinner after work at 6pm (as they call it) and proceed to his local watering hole to meet friends and pals to discuss business, politics and local interests.

He would quite likely enjoy a game of cricket and tennis His children would normally attend State or Private Schools. This is only one aspect of the British class system that from general observation and not really not trying to stereotype any one particular group. However due to new opportunities, education and social mobility the British class system is slowly fading and has become less prominent.

The English are normally quite reserved and this can be misinterpreted as being unfriendly but it is their nature to be discreet and unassuming. Unlike people from the Far East who are louder, more vocal and very expressive with lots of hand movements and gestures in their manner of speech, the English natives are much calmer in their mannerism and do not display their actual feelings. They do have a good sense of humour and at times use this as a shield to get along with people.

If you watch two Cantonese Chinese talking in public especially if they have not seen each other for a while -it's quite a drama!

I have also noticed that the English natives are generally well mannered, except for the few troublesome ones, whom some Teachers I have met in my supply teaching job, call them 'yabos'.

On the whole, I have found the English to be honest, polite, conscientious and patient. Culturally there are of course, differences, like it's a no, no to stroke a child's head, which is quite common in the East even among strangers.

Look into my eyes now, tell me what you see

To look into the eyes of the person speaking to you in England & UK is deemed honest but not in Asia, where it is considered rude and intrusive- even sexually suggestive.

People from the Far East, including myself, find it difficult to look into another person's eyes constantly whilst chatting. It is just not the custom, and nothing to do with being dishonest or have something to hide.

No wonder the Orientals appear shifty to the English!

In Jane Austen's novel, the person in her book character who open up too much, is viewed as not to be trusted The Romantic hero is resilient, reserved and should really not reveal too much.

Pitching to a new prospect who was the concert secretary of a social club, I thought my presentation was going really well. I was telling her quite a lot of my background - where I originate from the Far East, the cultural aspect of east & west and the many bands & duos I have been with- and that I am currently playing and performing three nights a week etc etc etc, when she stopped me in my track. During our conversation, I avoided looking at her eyes for a long period.

She gestured with her hands and said 'My Mum told me to be wary of people who share too much of their background and open up too much'

Guess she is a big Jane Austen fan, and have read Sense & Sensibility, cover to cover. It was a 'Hello, Goodbye'.

East meets West

The English in general are rather indirect in handling and approaching issues and do not want to appear too assuming, greedy or too eager. They also wear their emotional restraint as a badge of national pride. In the many schools I have worked in as a supply teacher, I have seen this first hand. If there are some cakes on the table, no one would want to dive straight in, to take the first piece. But eventually they all do gracefully!

'Isn't it a cold day' remarked Matthew, the supply teaching colleague during a break in between classes.

'Yes indeed, it is' I responded rubbing my hands.

'The Traffic was real bad this morning, were you caught in the massive jam?'

'No, I came in by another route' I said.

'It was atrocious, jam everywhere' he continued.

Walking towards the window, he exclaimed 'Oh my goodness, God, look at the amount of snow that is falling, we may be snowed in by this evening!'

'Oh no' I said.

'What are you doing weekend? He asked.

'Playing in St Helens with the band' I replied.

'Rock n roll and lots of boogeing all round and I am sure will be a good night. Wish I could come to see the band. ' Matthew said as he made a twisting movement with his burly body with both hands up.

'Yeah, it should be good' I responded, moving my comparatively tiny Chinese spare ribs body in a twist fashion, to mirror his, while sitting down.

Then walking towards me he raised his right hand to his mouth, two fingers touching his lips and asked quietly.

'Hey, could you possibly lend me a fiver?

Of course, this not typical of all English natives. Generally they are more reserved and would be more discreet. An Asian or Chinese would be more direct or even crude to the point.

Other interesting observations are the British do not shake hands as much as the people from the East. It is a normal practice for people from the East to greet each other with a handshake- either socially or in a business situation.

Very often at a gig this can be a great relief for me as I prefer not to shake hands with strangers as they offer their hands, for various reasons, especially if I am about to go on stage to play my guitar. Not to offend anyone, I would bow and say 'Let's do it the Eastern way-the Japanese style of greetings. ' It is also a good exercise for your backbones.

The instant exchange of business call cards which is so common and a huge part of eastern business etiquette. It is very normal for us to examine a given card for a while, before putting it away.

Also in western culture, silence in conversation is not a very comfortable thing from my observation.

Western culture of expression and empathy

There are various cultural differences I have noticed between East and West. I used to have quite a high voice back home but since arriving in England, I have tone down my voice. The slower measured expression is much preferred than one that come across as uncaring or careless or without consideration for the feelings of others.

Expressing sympathy upon hearing bad news

If an English man tell you his dear one has passed away it would not be appropriate to sign off the conversation on the phone with a high tone expression like we do in our Chinese style of speaking, like below.

'Oh really, I am so sorry to hear that, I will come for the funeral, BYE. eee!' in a high voice.

This would not indicate sadness but happiness, whereas saying it in a lower tone would convey a feeling of sad sorrow and empathy and will show you care.

What not to ask the English

What seems perfectly common questions from another culture may not be appropriate in the UK.

Avoid asking the English too much information about their personal lives, like we normally do back home when we are introduced to new people. Back home it is not too unusual to ask about someone's family background, their political views, their current relationship and even the value of their current property.

A definite no, no is asking how much they earn, the value of their property and at dining table (if they ever invite you / going out with them) avoid topics on sensitive topics like sex or politics, unless they bring it up or you know them extremely well.

'Hello Darling', or 'You alright Love'

You may be greeted by the English women in this manner for various services - when you are paying at the till.

Do not take it at face value that they really like you and want to be close to you.

In fact, all they are saying in actual fact is, 'will you just pay up and get out of here. I just want to get out of here too'

'Thank you Love'

This is just a native friendly greeting. The thank you part is a form of politeness and is sincere. Part and parcel of their polite culture but not so sure about the 'love' part!

'See you Love'

This is a common English way of wishing you on your way and hope to see you again. If it comes from a stranger or a supermarket cashier, they rather not see you again but is said to get you moving along and not hold up the queue.

'Hi Honey or Sugar Pie'

Another English way of being friendly or sugar coating you to make you feel warm and nice.

To get along fine with the native English people, you have to mirror their expressions and expectations.

A polite appreciation 'Thank you' and 'please' go a long way in Britain.

To eat is to prosper!

To Chinese, eating is a serious business and we focus on the food more than the people sitting around the table. In western society, conversation plays an important part and the eating is seen to be complimentary to it.

The first greetings we Chinese do when we meet each other back home in the Far East is to ask 'Have you eaten?' as opposed to the English weather conversational piece below:

'It is freaking cold today, ain't it?' or on a hot day . . .

'I am sweating like cobwebs' and if it is a really hot day . . . then it is 'bloody marvellous, ain't it?'

'Isn't it lovely today? The booming sun is out! Or it could be 'It's too flaming hot!'

To the Chinese to eat well is a good sign and to share the food with others is to show generosity and that gesture will in turn bring better fortune in the long run.

To say yes you have eaten in your response will indicate you are now prepared to face whatever adversity is thrown at you and you are ready to get on with the daily task. This goes back to the days of Chinese Coolie indentured labourers during the Colonial British rule of Singapore and Malaya where the labourers are fed by their Masters and would answer 'Yes, I have eaten' to signal the he ready to start work again, after his lunch break.

No. 8 & Red You are great but with no. 4 you are dead

When looking to buy a car I have noticed the salesman are nowhere to be seen-almost hiding somewhere, and screening to see if you are a serious buyer and sometimes prejudging you from the clothes and shoes you wear ! (as told to me by an English friend). This is my personal experience anyway and may not be totally representative of the rest.

In the Far East, the salesmen will be all over you before you even stepped out of your car! They are more hungry I suspect, than their more relaxed counterparts in England. Not forgetting there is no social welfare net if one is unemployed over in the East.

As a passing mention, it is a no go for a Chinese to buy any car number plate with the number 4. The number sound like death in Cantonese, Hokkien and Chinese dialects. The number 8 is the most preferred number as it means prosperity and 3 is also favoured as it is a reference to being very much alive and well.

Any Chinese worth his salt will not be seen dead driving with the car number 4 plate.

Red is Great!

As for colours the Chinese love red as it is a sign of prosperity and good luck. On the very opposite cultural end, a North Dakota University Research found the people who displayed anger were more likely to choose the colour red. Red colour for Chinese also signify good luck. And during the Chinese New Year Celebrations, Red packets is given out to the young children, unmarried adults either man or woman.

This is the tradition and Chinese custom in Singapore and Malaysia.

The affection for this bright colour (but discreetly used in western culture) is reflected in the National flags of China, Taiwan & Singapore –predominantly Chinese. Red is indeed great in the East! The Sun- life giver is red too!

Another Brick in the Wall

As an agency Supply Teacher in England, working in different state schools and special needs schools, have their challenging moments. One has to be on standby already in your suit and tie (John Lennon called it Monkey suit) from Monday to Friday. All ready to go awaiting the calls from the supply teaching agency.

There are days when the calls do not come, when all the Teachers are healthy and fit as a fiddle.

I can be a case of all dressed up and nowhere to go!

Supply Teaching work depend on teachers being off sick or absent on some other duties.

On my first assignment in a secondary comprehensive school, I found myself in a classroom full of very noisy and boisterous pupils. There was a pandemonium scene as I walked into the room. It was every school Teacher's nightmare. Pupils running around and things were being throw about paper planes, books went flying passed me, like a far reaching pershing rocket. There were many such incidents like this played out in a few more schools.

There was one where a student kept turning on the gas in the science lab and another who kept wanting to go to the toilet with another pupil. Suspecting they were just fooling about I asked in my Chinese slang 'Why, you two have diarrhoea?' which instantly brought the whole class down laughing. Till today I just don't know what is so funny about the question! It must be the way I said it. As a rookie Supply Teacher and being from a different background to all the English Kids, I was like a novelty and a subject of curiosity and at times a target.

There have been times when they practiced target shooting staples in my direction and have thrown objects when my back is turned to them. Hence, I always walked backwards facing them. This unusual walking style led one to ask me 'Sir, is that how you walk, back home?'

The kids in class in the Far East-China, Taiwan, Korea Singapore and Malaysia have a greater respect for their Teachers. In Japan they bow to their Teachers at the start of the lessons.

When I asked the English pupils their full names, the answers range from Ben Dover, Sally Clit to Robert Bogg. Trusting them and calling them during the class lesson by such names, drew an avalanche of laughter! I later checked the register after class and found no such names existed and through time, learned that they were 'having a laugh' as the native Teachers pointed out the meaning of such names to me, no doubt to my horror!

One good thing about supply teaching is you can choose not to go back to a particular school.

Of course, the behaviour of the pupils is not the general norm nor representative of the whole English Schools but I find such behaviour more prevalent in the more economically deprived areas. Majority of the schools-primary, secondary and special needs I have been to so far, have been pleasant.

In School, the pupils addressed me by my formal Chinese name and I am known to them as Mr. Yew.

Some lovely kids and pupils did drawings of me without my knowledge and so kindly gave it to me after lessons. It was such a lovely surprise and very touching!

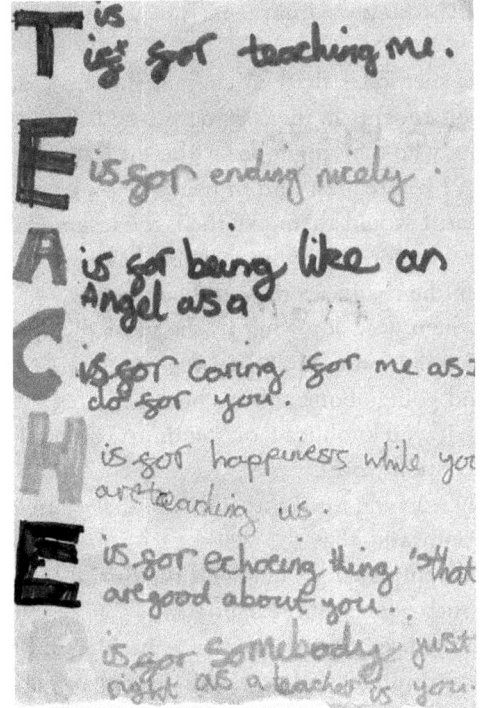

From Rachael Hannan Moston Primary School

Do you know Jackie Chan?

I have often been asked in Schools if I knew Jackie Chan. I don't know why but only the fact the English think we all look alike. Honestly, to me all the English do look alike, when I first arrived. I can honestly say 'I know nothing. ' But that has not stop me from using this, sometimes to gain favour with the kids especially the naughtier ones, when they asked me if I can bring them to meet Jackie Chan, I would grin and reply 'Ah, only if you do your work and behave today'

Of course it will be months or even a year when they see me next, as I will determine if I shall do supply work there again.

It only takes one very rowdy and uninterested child to create an unhealthy learning environment. And worst if there are two or a group.

There is a method I used to contain the most disruptive and rowdy child or students in the classroom.

Sussing out who that might be or who the leader of the pack is at the very start, I will request him or her to help me with the register. Following that, I would then give them the task and responsibility to keep an eye out for those who are misbehaving.

I have seen the change in these difficult pupils.

Without them even knowing it, the most disruptive and most mischievous pupil is now 'Mr. Somebody' on my side, trying to look important and going about bossing his classmates and shouting at them to 'Stop it, you knobhead' or ' Sit down you prat!' 'Shut it, will you' . . . alienation works!

On supply teaching duty, our role is to make sure there is order in the classroom and that the work set by the absent Teacher is explained and completed by all. I find the British kids are so fortunate to have such good school facilities.

Overall, it has been a good experience teaching in British Schools and the kids are a fun lot and generally well behaved in the majority of the schools.

In some remote parts in the third world countries, kids have to walk for hours to get to school.

I can still remember my primary school was very basic but we had good teachers and excellent sports activities and some basic facilities.

We used the outdoor field a lot for all kinds of sporting games and would recite religiously the timetable over & over again indoor.

$1 \times 2 = 2$, $2 \times 2 = 4$, $3 \times 2 = 6$ and so on, until it is basically ingrained in our tiny brains while growing up.

This method is called 'learning by heart.'

A recent press report in January 2014 indicated that British School Children are way behind their Far East counterparts internationally, in reading and writing.

In Mathematics Britain is 27th in World League as reported in 2014. I was shocked to know at first- hand that Teachers in England have been told not to mark down pupil's work and in some cases in red ink, as this may affect the motivation or morale of the pupil.

Personally, I feel the young at an early primary stage should learn to accept failure and take steps to help themselves and improve and regain the faith and confidence in themselves. This can be the first step and PTA, the Parent-Teacher Association and the School can play a major role as it should ideally be a joint effort by all and all those having responsibility for the children.

In Malaysia & Singapore the majority of children enjoy reciting their mathematics timetable, and also attend tuition after schools. A similar free tuition after school may help raise standards in say, Maths.

Having been to over 80 schools on supply teaching assignments in the North West England, I must say overall that there have been good standard of behaviour in the schools and with new buildings and better and spacious layout, the future looks bright!

Personally, having had the opportunity to work in the many different schools within the Lancashire and Greater Manchester areas, I have seen the need for more modern schools for the pupils, especially those in the deprived estates. New Schools are mushrooming with stylish designs to keep in pace with hi-tech 21st Century.

Also it is so satisfying to see former pupils doing well.

Have Guitar Will Travel

Whilst working in a School in Manchester on supply teaching assignment, I met two new members of staff Nick Jones & Simon Curran, both working as part-time musicians in a covers band.

This meeting led to me joining their group Flying Colours and after a couple of rehearsals we were out 'gigging' (playing) in local pubs.

Gig? What is it?

Until I came to England, I have never heard of the word 'gigging' which in musician language means performing. Back home Musicians would say we are doing a function but now the word 'gigs' is part of the vocabulary as the speedy internet connection and other sources spread the word around.

Europe and in particular England has exported the word 'gigs & gigging' to the Far East.

The Prime Minister of Malaysia, neighbour of the Island State of Singapore once directed his Youth and Sports Ministers to find out what the word 'Gig' meant to the Malaysian youngsters who were hanging out by the streets in the evening 'gigging.'

The hunt was on to find out what the youngsters were doing with this thing called 'gig'.

Curiosity kills the cat they say and so I did a little research on the internet and found that it was first used around the year 1225.

Following is an extract from The Word Detective online.

The first incarnation of "gig" around 1225, was to mean "a flighty, giddy girl," although this sense may well have been based on an earlier sense of "gig" meaning "something that spins or whirls" (as later found in "whirligig"). The Oxford English Dictionary suggests that "gig" may be onomatopoeic or "imitative" in origin, meaning that the word itself was meant to suggest something small that whirls. This sense of "gig" later came to also mean "an odd person, a fool" as well as "a joke" or "a state of boisterous merriment and fun ("*in high gig*"). *Another sense of "gig" appeared in the 18th century meaning "light one-horse carriage" perhaps based on the "bouncing, whirling" sense of the earlier "gig."*

The same word was later applied to a small boat used to ferry crew to a larger ship, and a small spear used to catch fish was also called a "gig," although the connection of this to other "gigs" is unclear.

Is it just me, or is this a lot like wandering through a darkened room, stumbling over furniture?

In any case, we now arrive at 1926 and the first recorded appearance of "gig" in print in the "musical engagement" sense.

The OED (and all other major dictionaries) label this usage as "origin unknown," but there seem to be two theories.

One traces this use to an earlier sense of "gig" meaning "a gambling bet" (possibly from the use of a spinning wheel in some original "gig" game), which then was generalized to mean "a business undertaking," and then applied to a musical performance.

The other, which I tend to favour, ties "gig" in the musical engagement sense to the original "spinning" meaning of the word, perhaps influenced by the Old French "gigue," meaning "dance," which also gave us "jig." Since playing at dances is how most musicians in history have made their livings, the use of "gig" to mean such a job makes perfect sense.

(Source from Internet: The Word Detective)

I now know what to do if someone ask me to explain the meaning of gig. It may be a good idea to print and have a ready hand-out on it.

After a couple of practices, I soon found myself on stage in various working men's clubs and pubs in England and Wales. I soon discovered that the dress code in clubs are more formal and they will usually have a changing room for the artistes and the majority of the clubs have long gaps between artistes' performance.

This gap is filled by members playing a game called Bingo. In this game, numbers are shouted out by the compere and patrons check to see if they have the same numbers in a row and they could win prizes normally in the form of money if they have a full house i. e. when all the numbers on the card are checked.

One interesting feature of the game is the compere calling out the numbers in a rhyming form for example, no 2 is one little duck (figure 2 looks like a duck) no 4 is knock at the door, no 8 is one fat lady - the figure 8 looks like a fat lady (according to the compere) number 11 is legs eleven (a pair of legs) and no 16 is sweet sixteen. I wonder what is no 10? One big hen? Join a band?

Usually there will also be a performance by the compere who doubled up as a resident singer, covering a wide repertoire of songs ranging from the fifties to the Sixties' music – mainly cabaret type.

In pubs the dress code is casual and the atmosphere is a lot noisier and boisterous. Traditionally pubs are watering holes, a sort of community meeting place.

Performing with English musicians have enriched my experience as a musician as there was so much to learn from observing good musicianship and the discipline that goes with it in the form of practice till perfect and the workings of the entertainment industry.

You don't drink! Eeh lad, What's wrong with thee?

When some of my English musician friends, patrons and Landlords of pubs found out that I don't drink beer or swear, don't gamble, don't take drugs, don't smoke, and only drink bitter lemon or ginger ale they were a bit surprised but understanding, after I explained that half a pint of lager or Guinness would get me drunk!

I have often been mistaken at gigs for anyone but a musician. A Kitchen porter, Health Inspector, a DVD Seller, a Cook, a doctor and even a spy!

There is a stereotype image of foreigners among the English natives especially of people of Chinese descent, but this is slowly changing with the times and when there is a lot more interaction among the various races.

For decades the Chinese and other foreigners of a certain racial origin seemed to be identified with a certain occupation and trades. Over the years as the younger generation received higher education and training, new opportunities opened up and today they are represented in other fields of work.

There was an occasion I was mistaken for a cook as I walked into a pub to get ready for setting up the band equipment. A member of the bar staff greeted me with a quick hello and said 'The Kitchen is that way.'

On other occasions, I have met with comments such as 'Do you have any DVDs in your bag?' or 'Oh my God, he is my family Doctor!' 'The Health and Safety man from the council is here.'

I can relate to the DVD identity as it was a common knowledge that all the fake DVD peddlers doing the pub rounds were illegal immigrants from China.

I now wear a flowery shirt, smart jacket and jeans and long hair and always walk in first with my guitar. The mistaken identity typecasting of a Chinaman has stopped. Now it's here comes the funky Chinaman!

After performing with various duos & bands all over the North West, we were often asked if we could recommend any good solo singers, duos or bands that we know of and seeking work in pubs and clubs.

Soon I started to introduce a few musicians I knew to the pubs and clubs and that triggered the idea of starting an artiste agency. From just two solo artistes till one hundred, Spectrum Agency is growing steadily.

Wonderful World Wide Web

'We can be on the moon or on mars, it really doesn't matter, as long as the Artiste gets to the venue and does a good job entertaining everyone that evening.' Replied the lady on the end of the phone line to my inquiry of where her agency is based. Her somewhat frank and honest reply got me thinking. Yes, why not, it does make sense in this high tech world we now live in. Everything is within a tap or click away!

I have been doing some research into the possibility of setting up an Artiste & Event Agency and looking into the workings of such a business venture. I started by speaking to people in the Industry, even calling up agencies pretending to book an act and finding out the procedures and fees and generally observing how the whole showbiz operate. What the Lady said was absolutely true.

In the current worldwide web world that we live in, the internet has made it possible to communicate and do business with anyone on planet Earth without leaving your front door or moving from the comfort of your seat and home.

A huge amount of time is saved in travelling, as in an instant, it is possible to send by email publicity materials and music CD Gigs Confirmation are emailed over to Artist and Client and even payment of agency commission by the Artiste is transacted and done online.

The wonderful world of mobile internet banking has arrived and revolutionised the world of business.

Wow, what an impressive 21st century technology!

Thank you, Sir Tim Berners–Lee, a British Genius and a Graduate of Oxford University, who invented the World Wide Web in 1989.

Dr. James Martin, another Oxford graduate is credited with predicting the internet in his 1978 work 'The Wired Society,' in which he wrote about how computers of the future would be linked up by phone-25 years before the internet became widespread.

The Accidental Artistes Agent

I came to England to work as a contract Supply Teacher in the secondary and special needs schools and starting a business especially one in the entertainment field was farthest from my mind. One can say, I am an accidental agent but passing on work to fellow musicians who are unemployed is a most satisfying feeling, when you hear they bought things for their kids, which they thought was not possible.

It's only a Click away
Let your fingers do the walking!

As the cheques and commissions started coming in, whilst I was on holiday in Rome, Sorrento & the Isle of Capri in Italy, I thought to myself, 'mmm . . . this looks like a possible and viable good business with income coming into the agency bank account whilst I am dressed in shorts, basking in the lovely sunshine and visiting museums and absorbing the Italian lifestyle! Mamamia!

Of course, it did not happen overnight. All those knocking on doors-cold calling on over 500 pubs and social clubs since for over 6 years have finally seen it's result. I am especially pleased when I passed on work to the unemployed musicians. It is a satisfying and rewarding experience, when you see them being happy and able to use their talent to improve their lives and that of their family.

The internet and mobile phone has made it possible to conduct a business anywhere, anytime and anyhow in any circumstances.

You can keep in touch at the touch of a finger! One can be walking on the road, sleeping in bed, watching television, lying on the hot beach, shopping and even making loaf (of bread), and continue taking bookings of artistes or chasing work, all at the same time.

The wonderful world of internet connects business with anyone on planet Earth without having to leave your front door or move from the comfort of your seat and home. A huge amount of time is saved in travelling, as in an instant, it is possible to send by email publicity materials and music CD.

Gigs Confirmation are emailed over to the Artiste and Client and more importantly, even payment of agency commission by the Artiste to the Agency is transacted and done online.

It was the most memorable moment of my life, when driving home one night after a gig a text message flash on my mobile . . . 'agency comm. just credited your bank account. Gig went well . . . on the way home, goodnight Radha'

The new speedy age of business has arrived and it is working wonderfully, by the click of a mouse!

Wonderful World of Online Banking

Agency comm transferred by mobile banking.

Good Gig…on way home. Good night Kee.
Cheers, Radha

25 horse riders @ 75 miles each –stopover 184 stations

Year 1860
Pony express mail service delivery by horseback
Missouri – California 1,900 miles - 10 days

Year 2015
Electronic Internet Banking Transfer
England –Singapore 6750 miles -3 minutes

Going Gigs Hunting

In the primitive cavemen days, people go out hunting not knowing if they will return alive with all the wild dangerous man-eating animals roaming freely, hungry and searching for food-just like them. With bravery and armed only with their net, stones and heavy wood objects they go out daily to the unknown.

Today it is so different and a lot safer. All we need is a pen, diary, map or a Sat Nav and lots of smiles and good gestures and a bit of luck when we go prospecting for sales and new business.

Along with these essential items would be added the promotional materials—posters, artistes profiles and their photos and their music CDs etc. plus throwing into the car compartment a packet of mint, a mars bar, a yellow banana for foods on the road.

As kids out playing after school, I used to send a monkey up the coconut tree to pluck and throw them lovely coconuts down—for all my friends waiting in anticipation for the monkey trick! The coconut water is just delicious especially in the very hot and humid climate of Malaya and Singapore. The rewards are the ground nuts for the monkeys, when they descend. This was my early year's entrepreneurial spirit!

To achieve the one hundred artistes target in the Artiste Agency, Spectrum-Ktbg, I drew a plan to visit and call on at least ten pubs a day. It is an exhaustive hunting journey, stopping, getting out of the car and walking into the unknown, but I know unlike the caveman, I will come out alive!

It was a bitterly cold day as I drove into the empty car park of the Red Lion pub. I parked and looked around, gazed up the building of the premise, hoping for someone to appear at the window but no sign of life, not a soul was in sight.

Like the lions and the graceful tigers that go out for their prey and food hunting, I had to wait patiently.

It is said good things come to those who wait and that patience is a virtue. I guess I acquired patience from my calm and loving parents.

I recall a journey my brothers, I and our Father made travelling from Kuala Lumpur to the East Coast State of Kelantan, near the border of Thailand.

The roads then were narrow and winding through thick Malayan Jungle, and crossing ferries from one point to the next was normal and dangerous at times.

My Father, a gentle tall six footer (unusual for any Chinese) was Sales Manager for the American Oil Company, Caltex Oil Corporation and had to travel frequently to the East Coast States to develop new petrol stations -in the newly Independent Malaya.

Live Malayan Tigers at play!

On this particular journey on a hot afternoon, we waited for more than an hour in our car, as it was blocked by a family group of Malayan tigers, on the narrow road winding around the thick jungle trees, leading to Kuantan, a small coastal town of East Malaya.

Though we were very excited and intrigued with the lovely tigers in front of us, it was hot in the car and we were all impatient and hungry, but our Father told us to be very quiet and wait patiently as we should not disturb the animals, in case they get aggressive.

Sure enough for over an hour we were entertained with a tiger show- lots of plays, growling, lying and walk about by these beautiful stripy animals.

Being patient does have its rewards, and this fatherly advice always stay with me for the rest of my life.

Fast forward to the car park of the pub in the winter of England. Sitting in the car waiting, whilst keeping my ears and eyes open for any sign of life within the pub, I started to go through my list of prospects (pubs, clubs, hotels, restaurants, promoters etc.) and made my first of the daily one hundred calls routine. I am constantly on the phone, like a phone-maniac (is there such a word? Maybe I should patent this word! Like 'Beatlemaniac' 'vodkamaniac'.

It's important and can be quite rewarding albeit at times frustrating to the point of infuriating when making these calls.

The calls I make are divided into strong leads, follow up and

Going Gig Hunting

cold calling and prospecting for work for my agency artistes and the bands I am playing with (last count I was in six different groups–Duos, Trios & Bands.)

I got my training in constant phone prospecting new businesses from my training in a college back home where I was constantly on the line calling prospects and later promoted to Team Leader, responsible for a team of college employees phoning and talking to prospective students and their parents about the courses offered by the college.

We had to target at least a hundred calls per day per employee. It was tiring, testing and challenging.

Daily in England quite a lot of people gets unsolicited phone calls and texts from numerous companies and it seems to be a numbers game. Out of a 100 calls I make daily, the positive response rate is about 15 percent.

The local accents posed a challenge and daunting task to me. Many a times the Landlord can't make out what I am saying and vice versa. I struggle to understand the Liverpool and other Irish accents and often would spell out the words to move forward. It's A for apple, R for Romeo and O for Orange and B for Banana.

This is how I manage the conversation at times. Still, it's a good start.

On one of my pub cold calling rounds after school, I found this particular pub closed. Going round the back of the pub, I heard the loud sound of a lawnmover but could not see anyone due to the high wooden fencing.
Not deterred, I knocked 3 times on the wooden panels and shouted 'hello' and this Gentleman came peering over the fence.
As I was trying to shoot a cloud image of a horse in the sky above, I captured the moment he appeared in my apple mobile photo frame !
After explaining the reason for my calling, the kind chap let me in to see the Landlady and got a booking for the band. What a Kind of a Guy ! Kind & helpful !

Over The Fence

I found out the best times to call pubs for work are between 11am – 1pm and 3pm- 5 pm when the pubs are quieter, as it is in the morning the landlord has to do the banking and getting the premise ready for opening.

As I made the many daily calls in my car, I kept looking up to the pub building hoping to catch a glimpse of any sign of life especially of the landlord. Suddenly I saw the twitching of the curtains and there was a figure in the upstairs window of the pub.

Not so long after this, a lone figure approached my car cautiously and I noticed that his eyes were fixed on me. He asked if I was there to see somebody. Slowly unwinding the car window I replied, 'Yes, I am here to see the Landlord. '

'I am the landlord, what seems to be the problem?' he replied, looking at me with some caution.

In England, a landlord is the person who is in charge of and has the responsibility of running a pub.

'Oh hello, can I see you regarding recommending you my Band and some excellent Artistes for your pub?'

I asked, as I greeted him with a big smile and extending my hand for a friendly handshake.

After showing him the portfolio of the Artistes and my band, the reassured landlord confided that he was at first apprehensive when he saw me from the upstairs.

According to him my presence at that time looked rather suspicious, especially when parked up behind the pub at that time of the morning. Monday morning, the first day of the week is when pubs does its bank deposit from the weekend takings of Friday Saturday & Sunday.

A word of advice to anyone going gigs hunting - avoid parking behind the pub premise and waiting in the car at 9 30am, first thing Monday morning. Not an ideal start!

I started my artiste agency with only two artistes – Frank Forde, a Frank Sinatra Tribute Act and a Tina Tribute Artiste, presented by Janet James.

Frank Forde from Stockport, Manchester, is a very well-known North West England Entertainer who has performed with many of the Giants of the Industry famous names like the man with the golden voice, Matt Monroe, Comedian Bernard Manning, Frank Carson, the Legendary Bill Haley and the Comets and a variety of Stars from the fifties and sixties era.

Frank Forde bless his heart, always never fail to send me a handwritten note of thanks whenever he sends the agency commission after his gig engagement.

I would go cold calling pubs in different towns after my supply teaching work normally after school around 4pm. This is the ideal time to call on pubs to hunt for work- as it's generally quiet, and Landlords are more likely to have some spare moment during this so called 'happy hours.'

Back home we have this time frame called 'the happy hours' between 3-5pm, where drinks and food are served at a generous discount rate.

The other ideal time to call is between 10-1pm before the pub gets busy for the lunch crowd.

As most pubs do not open until about 11am, I find the most practical way is to go round the back of the premise and knock on the windows or ring the doorbell. Many a time, I would encounter delivery vans and the delivery men would be the key to gain entry to meet the landlord or the manager of the business. In the event no one is in, I would normally leave a calling card or get a contact number from the delivery man.

Cold calling 500 Venues.

I must have visited over five hundred pubs, clubs, cafes and restaurants over the years. This is one advantage of supply teaching being sent to a different school in different areas each week. After school at 3 30pm, I would cold call on the pubs near the schools, in different areas, looking to secure work.

Driving past pubs I would often look for the A board or posters on pub windows with 'Live Music' signs.

I have noticed that whenever I walked in, all the customers heads will turn towards me and all eyes will be trained on me. I think they are puzzled what this Oriental in a suit & tie want, at this time and place. In a suit and tie holding a folder, I stood out from the crowd and have been mistaken for a Health & Safety Inspector, a Tax & Enforcement Officer, a Doctor, Lawyer -anyone but a Musician.

The Landlords are generally welcoming and it's more out of curiosity that they are eager to hear what this Oriental looking guy is trying to say and what goods or services he has up his sleeves

In the beginning it took quite a bit of convincing, and a few more visits as I was a total stranger but the perseverance paid off and soon the band got a couple of engagements followed closely by the artistes .

A pub has been described as 'homely place full of homely characters.'

Asked do you need a comedian? The landlord retorted, 'Do I need a comedian? 'There is a room full of them here already, and I can't shift them fast enough!' pointing in the direction of a group of smiling men in the corner of the pub.

Today Spectrum-ktbg supply acts to over one hundred pubs in the North West and throughout UK.

The road to achieving the one hundred pubs target was a long and difficult one in the face of strong competition and economic downturn.

In all my rounds to the hundreds of pubs, the native English have shown me kindness and for that I am grateful for their support in providing work to the agency artistes and bands.

There have been some negative reporting about the unruly patrons at pubs and clubs. In all the almost 300 venues I have worked with all the past ten years, there has only been a handful of incidents-all minor ones.

Besides, the presence of the CCTV cameras inside and outside of the premises, have significantly deterred crime.

The Good, the Bad, the Ugly & the Uglier

In my rounds of cold calling on over 500 pubs after school hours the past 6 years, I have met many pleasant landlords. For the benefit of the readers back home in Singapore and Malaysia, the people running the pubs are called Landlords and others are licensees or paid to run the business as Managers. Not getting too technical about the terms in this book, I shall refer to them as Landlords or Managers running it on behalf of a large group of companies or the Brewery.

The Good were the Landlords/Managers who were encouraging and would honour the gigs booked, even in difficult circumstances where the takings were poor that evening, but the band or singer got paid in full as agreed.

The Bad experience are those acts who did a good show but ended up not fully paid by the venue due to low turnout and below the expected earnings at the till.

The bad are also those landlords/managers who rang to cancel the bookings one day or a couple of hours before the gig date, giving little time for alternate bookings to be arranged for the artistes or bands.

The Ugly are the ones that gives you a booking but do not bother to inform you they have left the pub and when the artiste or group turned up, find the venue closed or the new landlord has no idea of the booking.

The Uglier are the ones that enticed you to come to their premise or ask you to keep calling with promise of work for musicians and then agreed on the phone the booking dates and say he would need the posters soon but when you arrived, he has apparently left for New York!

And Uglier still are those agencies that send people round to try to discourage your artistes or entice them to join their agencies. Without realising it, I have over the years taken some business from the other established agencies. This is what free enterprise and competition is about.

The Clients were attracted to my agency's provision of free colour posters for all artistes booked, free 100 flyers and online social media promotions.

I hold no ill feelings towards the Ugly and Uglier ones except to say that the Good people I have met override the Bad, and they make living in England a more pleasant experience.

Hello! Is it me you are looking for? 100 calls a day.

Many musicians have commented how I was always gigging even in bad economic times, when pubs are closing down all around- like a collapsing deck of cards!

There is no short cut to finding work. The constant daily 100 (50 in the day and 50 at night) calls I make to pubs and new prospects has resulted in continuous work for the bands I am playing with and for the agency's artistes.

Smile, you are a CCTV Star!

Everywhere you go in the UK, from the minute you walk out of your house and every step you take, till you return home, you are being constantly watched by all the CCTV cameras installed in almost every corner of the UK. Then there are the very concerned members of the British public-the walking CCTVs. A survey report state revealed there is one surveillance camera for every eleven persons in Britain.

There are CCTV cameras everywhere, in petrol station, town centres, eateries, shops and shopping malls, and on the buses, trains and trams and motorways. It does seem Big Brother is watching and monitoring your every move twenty-four hours a day, round the clock. There are up to six million CCTV surveillance cameras in the UK according to a report by the British Security Industry Association.

It has been reported that a person is filmed on CCTV camera for at least thirty times a day. On the other hand the advantage of such surveillance, unwelcoming as it may be, and somewhat an intrusion into one's privacy, has its benefits especially in combating crimes.

Quite a many common criminal acts and even murders have been solved and those committing them have been apprehended because of evidence from such security surveillance and the tips from members of the public.

In many Far East Asian Countries such evidence are not available or forthcoming and not a common thing, making it harder to combat crime.

What I find sad about the state of British society is its political correctness and fear culture. The level of suspicion directed at adults whenever they interact with children is most unwarranted and despairing.

In other foreign cultures, especially the Far Eastern countries, the children mix easily with the adults and stroking a stranger's child's head is a sign of friendly affection. In England children's playground, high alert will be raised if any adults especially strangers are present where children are playing around. Of course, one has to be careful about strangers with bad intention approaching children, but common sense should prevail.

I recall an incident when I was visiting Fleetwood and stopped to take some photos of a bandstand up in the distant hill that look quite interesting to me at that time. Lo and behold, I had a visit from the local 'Bobby' a few days later, asking me if I had been to Fleetwood over the weekend and taking photographs there. I replied proudly 'Yes, of course, I take photos all the time wherever I go. I like to record my stay in England and show to family and friends back home' He then asked me further.

'Did you take photographs of some children up in the hill?'

I was astounded by his question and asked if there was a problem.

The Officer said, 'A member of the public has made a complaint that you have been taking photos of children playing up on the hill.'

I was shocked and burst out laughing,

'Really? Oh my goodness, I can't believe this, Officer. ' I said, shaking my head.

Upon request from the officer, I showed him the images that I took, explained to him that being a foreigner in England, I like to record the places and people I visited. He was satisfied that there was no ulterior motive as the children's images can hardly be seen in the photos that were taken from a far distance.

Whilst I find this amusing at that time, it does hit home that in Britain a fear culture has descended upon the society wherever it involve children in so many different situations.

As for my close brush with the law with regard to the photo in question. It happened when I was focusing on what looked like a bandstand, when suddenly a group of children appeared and rolled down the hill, as I snapped the image. They then waved at me while running around and shouted something incoherent, and like my jolly friendly self, I waved back at them.

Days later a police officer waved at me to stop as I was about to drive off to work. Ha! Ha!

The Photograph that nearly got me into trouble with the law

I took this photo of the unique looking building in Fleetwood to add to my UK Album.

Tale of Harry Ho Ho Ho & away he goes to Harrods!

A friend of my friend, Harry Ho related an unpleasant encounter on his visit to London with his family with an over 'Enthusiastic child protector and Guardian of public interests' (ECPAGOPI as I call them). They are what some may call busybodies or what I nicknamed as the 'Walking CCTVs.'

At a busy zebra crossing his five year old child was playing up and Harry like Harry the dad back home, then decided to discipline the child there and then by pulling his ears and smacking him on the hand – a tried and tested Chinese discipline over the years gone by.

My friend was somewhat taken by surprise at the sudden appearance of a tall and burly English gentleman, who reprimanded him for doing so.

'Goodness, who do you think you are, stopping me from disciplining my own son?' Harry asked.

'I am a concerned member of the public and what you just did to the child is wrong and you can be charged for child cruelty' came back the reply,

'Oh really' Harry shot back, 'Mind your own business.'

'Not when you are hurting the little boy' he responded angrily, with some authority in his voice.

Harry then challenged him by asking, 'So what are you going to do about it?'

'I'm going to report you to the authorities for child cruelty and mistreatment of a child' he added.

'Go ahead' Harry said, quickly marshalling his whole family to move on and walked away quickly.

The man was soon on the phone trying to report Harry whilst following them round the block. Harry was trying to shake him off from following and walked his family into different alleys and corners of building. He had a vision of being surrounded by a team of police from Scotland Yard, being handcuffed and taken away to spend a night in the cell. What a story this would be to tell friends when he returns home.

Trying a last attempt to lose the well-meaning and conscientious 'Stalker' he then decided to enter the prestigious Harrods and it was in this vast store that Harry finally managed to get away.

What a relief and what an experience for a tourist in good old London!

From these tales, it does seem that children in Britain are given the highest priority in their welfare and protection and some people can be over zealous in trying to prevent child abuse.

Still it is best practiced with common sense.

Of course, the welfare of the child is of paramount importance but Parents from my part of the world, may be astonished as Harry Ho did in his encounter with an ECPAGOPI my own invented abbreviation for overeager, over 'Enthusiastic Child Protector and Guardian of Public Interests.'

Beside their well-meaning laws on the protection of young children, the other trait I found in English people is their love & care for the animals. They have a soft spot for and kind to our furry friends. Awww!!!

Awww ... is an expression which shows the soft side of the British people who love their pets- I never heard this expression till I came to England. Aw!!! How lovely and sweet it really is!

The British have a special place in their hearts for dogs from my general observation beside other pets.

I saw her standing there.

One summer afternoon whilst I was driving, I saw a Lady standing in the middle of the road. Curious to find out why she was doing so and being concerned for her welfare & safety, I stopped and asked her.

'Hi, are you alright?'

Looking somewhat happy to see me, the Lady pointed to something between her legs.

'Yes, but I am a bit worried for this little hedgehog in the middle of the road' she replied.

This is the very first time I have seen a hedgehog live!

'What is that?' I asked rather curiously.

'A Hedgehog.' She said proudly.

'I know, but what is that between your legs? 'I asked again, rather more curious.

'A Hedgehog! She shouted back. You don't know what is a Hedgehog? She asked looking at me with a surprise look and pointing to it.

At last I see the cute creature-looking like a fruit I know back home the Durian, a spiky green coloured fruit. 'Yes I see it now' I said to her.

'Aw poor thing' … I sounded emphatically.

Until I came to England I have never heard anyone expressing this Aw … thing …the English do have a soft side!

Mahatma Gandhi once remarked that the greatness of a Nation and its moral progress can be judged by the way its animals are treated

Soon a kind soul came passing by and offered to pick the hedgehog up and place it on a safer path.

I offered a quick advice without much thinking it through 'Give it a gentle kick along till it reaches the safe side of the road' I said to the shocked look of the kind considerate lady. 'You can't kick the poor animal. That would be cruel!' she responded looking rather angry and upset at my 'expert' suggestion. I guess she is right.

I can visualize the press headline 'Nasty Chinaman kicked hedgehog like a football disgusting.'

Frankly, I have not the slightest clue how to handle with care the tiny cutie, except to perhaps, pick it up and gently put it down in a safe place.

That's exactly what a blonde kind soul did.

Hallelujah! It all ended well with a photo opportunity of the kind lady and the little cute prickly creature. Altogether now … Aww!

It is quite clear that in England and the UK as a whole, it must be noted that the English care tremendously for the welfare of animals and children.

To all my friends, relatives and visitors from the Far East you have been warned!

Happy Together

There is a long and well known unwritten rule that the customer is always right and is King.

Today with price wars among the supermarkets in England, the Customer is the Master of the Universe.

In 1909 when the first Selfridges opened for business, the slogan 'The Customer is always right' was banded about and rolled out in promoting the concept that the interest of the customer is at the heart of Selfridges.

They tweaked Swiss Hotelier, Cesar Ritzi's 'The Customer is never wrong.'

Each time a booking is confirmed, it is a good idea to find out the type and profile of the Customers who patronise the venue-age group, genre of music preferred and any special occasion.

Selecting the right act for the right venue is crucial to a successful evening for all. As at the end of the evening it would be a wonderful feeling to know and see that everyone had a jolly good time and went home with a big smile on their face!

Can you play Satisfaction? Can I Sing?

Sometimes patrons come along to ask Musicians to play a certain song on the spot and if they don't, the patrons feel disappointed but bands cannot be expected to play perfectly on request.

Getting the patrons dancing should be the yardstick for all Artistes and Bands to gauge how successful the evening has been.

I often encouraged patrons (those sober enough) to come up to join in the singing at some point in the set. I remember the not so stable Gentleman who was zigzagging towards the band blurring out a song and shouting out 'Let me sing, let me sing!'

The poor chap fell down before he could reach the mike stand.

Audience participation is fun and this generally will create a sing-along and would often lead to a group of dancers taking to the floor in a round of merrymaking!

Got to be starting something!

I would often check out the patrons in the venue and there would be the usual familiar faces. On any first time visit to a new venue it's always good idea to break the ice by saying hello to the patrons who have arrived early and getting to know their names or even finding out if someone is celebrating something that evening so that a certain rapport can be started when on stage later …

'Hello, Jimmy & Irene over there who are celebrating their wedding anniversary this week, let's give them a big cheer…hip hip hooray!

And …

'To Caroline & friends sitting in the corner, have a wonderful holiday in Greece next week!'

'It's Julie's birthday today everyone …' and the Band break into the Happy Birthday song accompanied by almost everyone present.

In almost all occasions following such greetings there would be a buzz around the room and the people that you just wished and all in the room will almost instantly respond by clapping, making some kind of noise and in most cases they would be the group that will initiate the move to the dance floor, and soon you have others following and casting aside any inhibitions and dancing away!

It's really all about them

There is nothing more disheartening than a Singer or band playing to an empty room. Performers feed off the applause of the audience.

It's the feeling of being recognized and appreciated as Musicians. Patrons of any pubs like being recognized and appreciated too by the performers.

They want to feel that they are getting good value for their money, and they want to feel that they have had a really good evening and being entertained.

All the musicians I have worked with know that I often extend a song, especially if there are people just coming up to dance, just when the band is into the last verse of the song. There is nothing so disappointing than for two people or more who are about to enjoy a dance, when the music is coming to an end. It is like an anti-climax!

The general idea is that at the end of the evening, the Landlord is happy and believed that he has got value for money, the Band or Artiste performed well and the Customers had a really good time –and everyone went home happy and chirpy!

Happy Patrons

Chopsticks, Tigers & Chips

Shout Out Loud!

To bring more people into the pub it is important that efforts in promoting the event by way of mouth, local posters, internet, local papers, radio, banners are well organised.

To stay competitive, I often provide free as part of the service, 200 flyers and some posters of A4 and A3 size to pubs and clients when they agree to take a 6 months contract with my agency. I would personally distribute the flyers door to door to homes in the locality of the venue.

Hence if there is a celebration of some sort either birthday or anniversary it will definitely lift the spirit of the evening and bring more people to the evening event.

In times of economic downturn, pubs are facing a very difficult trading period and if we can bring in an extra ten new patrons it will no doubt be adding extra cash for the business and keep live music going.

There are a few popular online social media sites & channels which one can exploit for promotion and publicity such as Vimeo, Twitter, Flickr, YouTube, Weibo, northwest bands, Facebook, Whatsapp, Youtube and the free local publications. Word of mouth is free publicity.

Agency- Client Relationship

It has been said that running a business is like riding a bicycle. The minute you stop you are likely to fall down. Keeping in contact with clients and especially prospective ones are all important aspect of any business. Working from my car and home, I am constantly on the phone daily making at least a hundred calls prospecting for work and the Client know they can speak to me anytime.

It's not uncommon to receive calls from pub around 11 30pm requesting for next day booking. Obtaining feedback on how an act went the previous night and following up on hot leads are all part of the process of keeping in touch with existing clients and developing new business.

Gosh, what is his name again?

Trying to remember English names can be daunting at times, when you have been performing in and out of over a hundred pubs & clubs, so I often write them down or key it into my mobile the name of the landlord, concert secretary or manager with the name of the of the venue next to it.

Sometimes I even add in the name of their spouse, children and pets and would earn praise from them that I have such good memory and so considerate! Imagine the reaction when I ask about their family on the phone naming their pet and family! My goodness, how do you ever remember all the names after all these months and years? You must have a fantastic memory!' exclaimed the surprised Landlord not knowing I have keyed the names into my mobile or written it down in a notebook.

People like hearing their names called out -it's the sweetest sound and thing to their ears! It might appear discourteous if they remember yours and you don't, when you turn up at the next appointment. There have been situations when they greeted me by calling out my name as I strolled in and start to introduce me to their customers and their spouses.

And I am standing there, not being able to return the kind compliments by addressing the Landlords by their names as I cannot remember it -totally cannot recall their names at that very moment! So I would deploy the tactic of 'Oh, do introduce yourselves' to the band members pretending to be busy putting away the equipment that we brought into the pub. In that way, I save the embarrassment of not remembering their names as they proudly say out their names when they introduced themselves to one another.

Sometimes I employ the tactic 'Hi, it is really nice to see you again, How do you spell your name? After they have written out their names, I would hold the paper and go ' Isn't there another way of spelling or isn't the short form of Michael, Mike?' This often generally works and I get to know his name then.

Whenever I go out 'gigs hunting ' or to use the appropriate business word 'prospecting' for work for the band or artistes, I would after the presentation drop a link to my name, so its memorable and not forgotten easily. 'If you lose your house or car key remember me' or 'if you ever go to Singapore or Kuala Lumpur let me know and if I happen to be there, I will show you round. '

To improve the relationship with the Client, I always keep in touch with them via email, phone and personal visits. It is always a good idea to patronise your Client's business, whenever possible.

When I learned that a landlady client of my agency had been hospitalised, she was surprised that I turned up with some fruits and a card to wish her speedy recovery. On her return, she gave the agency more work-not that I was expecting her to do so.

Supporting the venue & getting feedback

I believe that artistes should always support the venues and would advise the pubs not to offer the Artistes any complimentary drinks but let them pay, as without them operating profitably, there would be no work for the Musicians. I would request them not to say I said it.

As a general rule, I would call them up to find out the response of the patrons to the Singers sent the previous night. The best feedback and real feedback is not from the Artiste but the Client & Customers.

The pubs today are struggling to keep their business open and especially so in these difficult and trying times of the world financial crisis.

Cheap beer prices sold in supermarkets and the non-smoking ban are two of the reasons often quoted among others as contributing to the closing of this very British tradition and institution.

The Times they are a Changing

The pub landscape has changed dramatically since the year 2000. The impact of the financial crisis, trading practices and legislation has hit hard on the trade and led to the current dire situations.

I have personally seen the hardship inflicted. June 2014 press reported UK pubs are closing at a rate of 1, 612 a year. Two pubs a week are converted to supermarkets.

In 1946 there were close to 73, 000 pubs in Wales and England. In 2010 there remain 52, 000.

Some have been converted into banks, cafes, flats, mini supermarkets, and quite a few are even Mexican hair removal clinics. Some are now postal collection centres!

Thou shall not drink!

Ironically at this very moment of typing, one of my local pubs is being converted into a place of worship! Thou shall not drink? Guess it is one of the ways, the power above, convert the unrepentants!

To help bring in more customers and to keep the pub business viable is a joint effort of both the Government and all involved in the Industry.

As a sign of appreciation to the pubs for engaging the bands or artistes, I always request friends and members of the band or the Artiste booked for a particular venue to encourage everyone they know to come on the night of the performance.

For a new landlord taking over a pub poses lots of challenges. And for the live entertainment it is a question of Who, Where and How to revive live music again.

Very often new landlords would want to settle down first before organising live entertainment. Therefore, it is not unusual for the new takeovers to cancel all gigs booked by the previous Landlords.

I would often propose a few ideas to kick start the live entertainment and one of the most effective one is to introduce jam or free mike sessions, to try to draw in the crowd. The casual 'free and easy' jam night or more popularly known as open mike sessions will be a magnet and a convenient place for local musicians.

In the next chapter, I would like to share some personal experience on how to resolve certain issues, pertaining to bookings with pubs and social clubs.

We Can Work It Out
Singer vs Karaoke- The pros and cons

A common issue and occurrence in current economic climate. Some pubs feel it is cheaper to put on for the entertainment, a karaoke or DJ. I would try to justify the benefit of a live act and the drawing power and entertainment value for it. I would impress upon the Landlords that they will be given support in the form of posters and publicity materials for the promotion and will encourage the Artiste or Band to invite friends along on the night. Inviting five friends will be an extra five new patrons spending at the bar.

Obviously Karaoke has its own attraction and value as people like to hear their lovely voices 'belting' out their favourite numbers, they have been practicing all week in the toilet or whilst out driving in the car. The biggest plus factor is all your pals can join in the fun!

Cancellations
What to do in such an event?

The call that all musicians especially those who are solely depending on the income dread. A call to say the venue has to cancel the booking.

If the booking is through an agency and depending on the circumstances and reasons for the cancellation, there is recourse for legal action and compensation. In the absence of a valid contract, the chances for recovery of loss earnings are slim but not totally hopeless-if it can be proven some verbal agreement was in place.

In one case it was proven by text that there was some agreement in place between the pub and the band and the posters were put up to promote the act and in the social media and the cancelled gig resulted in loss of income from another venue which wanted to book the band. Again, proof is needed.

The best alternative is to find another gig to replace it. There is very little one can do short of suing the landlord –which can be unfruitful, time consuming and costly.

But a local county court action is not all that difficult to pursue or really complicating.

County Courts or small claims courts deal with all types of civil action, which can include personal injury, family issues, discrimination, employment disputes and financial and housing disputes.

In England and Wales there are three main types of small claims, known as tracks.

Depending on the nature of the claims, a decision will be made to which claim track should be used.

» Small claims track - £5, 000 or less

» Fast track - £5, 000 - £15, 000

» Multi-track - £15, 000 – 50, 000

The claim must be made to the County Court within six months of the day of the incident, otherwise it may not be possible to proceed to make a claim.

In serious cases, an extension may be given on the time limit.

- ***How to start a County Court Action.***

    1. Seek the advice from your Solicitor, your local Citizens Advice Bureau. Go Online: www.justice.gov.uk or www.county-courts.co.uk

    2. Fill in the relevant claim form.

    3. Pay the required fee from £25 onwards (money claim online) for a claim up to £300. Check fees under Court fees chart. You will be able to claim back, if you win but pay all costs if you lose the case.

The Court will write to the Defendant and if claim is challenged a date for hearing will be set.

In the meantime, it may be worth trying a mediation service – where an impartial person helps to work out an agreement satisfactory to both sides.

- ### *Change of management/ownership of the pub/club*

Turning up at a venue to find it all boarded up and closed, or the new management were not expecting an act that evening, is the one of the worst scenario, but it does happen to musicians-not an amusing thing!

Again very little can be done except to phone round to see if another venue would like to engage a band/artiste at the very last minute for a discounted rate. It may be worth trying to contact the head office to pursue the matter to claim for expenses, if not the full amount of the engagement.

Always handy to have phone contact of pubs at hand just in case you need to call other venues if this happened. I once sent a band to another venue after they found themselves in such a situation. Frantically calling round, I managed to secure another booking nearby to the closed venue, with only an hour to spare before they were due on stage.

Thanks to my brand new Apple mobile phone and the time honoured slogan of the yellow pages 'Let your fingers do the walking' did wonders. Technology and contacts saved the day.

- ### *Client / Landlord not happy with the Act*

To avoid such a situation, it is best to find out exactly what is expected and get close to matching what is required.

Artiste not adhering to the terms of the agreement e. g specified & advertised time of performance and type of music expected by patrons.

Good communication between all parties and abiding by the terms and conditions is important.

- ### *Poor turnout on night band /singer was on*

Pubs & Clubs and the Agency are responsible for the promotion of the live events in their venues.

The Act booked should ideally shout out loud to all friends and supporters to come along to support them to make the evening a success, and in the process get a rebooking.

I would as a standard feature of the service of the Agency supply the venues with publicity posters and place them in all the prominent positions within the pubs and on their windows and promote the acts appearing there by way of flyers and through other social media. The Venue is obliged to pay the agreed amount to the Acts regardless of the turnout, as per the contract.

- ***Client/pub landlord not entirely satisfied with the Act and want a discount on Artiste fee***

Depending on the circumstances of each gig, it is always best to find out exactly what are the reasons and given the right reasons, to allow a discount.

- ***Client not happy - stop Artiste & send Artiste home***

Again vetting each Artiste before sending them on any booking is essential- to weed out the new and inexperienced and mediocre standard performer.

The Artiste should always arrive early to set up in good time. This will also ease any concerns the venue may have had and also to the patrons, who will be assured that there will be a live performance-hence not leaving.

But it is at the discretion of the Client to stop an Artiste if the Act is not up to his expectations and a suitably agreed amount is paid to the Artiste.

Client bypasses Agency and hires Artiste directly

Artistes are all self-employed and they choose who they like to work with and it's totally their privilege.

The Agency's Gig Confirmation and the contract spells out clearly the Client's legal obligation to engage the service of the Agency for any future rebooking of Artiste and the Band, within a certain stipulated period.

The legal obligations stated will usually be a good basis for any action for recovery in a court of law.

- ***Objections from Residents***

Some pubs face objections and have restricted time for live music following complaints from nearby residents.

It would be a good move to invite the nearby residents to a meeting to resolve any complaints and to take steps to reduce the noise level.

Putting in a noise control unit -where the power supply is cut off, once certain noise decibel level is reached is a useful system to install in the premise, as a possible solution. The limited restrictions cut off power at 103-104 Decibels.

Another positive action the pub landlord can consider is to invite his immediate affected residents to a meet or write them outlining what measures are being put in place, to reduce the noise level.

Majority of Councils in England & Wales prefer the win-win formula, where licensed entertainment venues, near residential estates, stop loud live music at a certain time, usually 11pm. They do eventually realise the impact a ban will have on the earnings of the venues and the loss of earnings of the musicians. If representations are made it can be a good outcome.

- ***Agency-Artiste Relationship***

Right from the start of the agency, I was determined to cultivate, build and maintain good relations with each and every Artiste and Band on the roster of Spectrum Agency. The process of building trust and confidence is helped by the fact that being a musician myself I do empathise reasonably well with all of them.

Each Artiste is self-employed and rightly so, as they can decide if they wish to accept work in a certain venue and they basically set the pace for the number of gigs they wish to do.

Even though there exist in place a contractual working relationship between the Artiste and the Agency, it works better if it is based on 'absolute good faith.'

A mutually respectful ties will result in all the concerned parties agreeing to resolve issues and avoid conflicts.

As the pub business is volatile and cancellations are common, both Agency & Artiste should work together to find alternate solutions, thus bypassing any unpleasant situation that may arise.

I always try to find alternate work for the Artiste, in the event of a cancellation either solo work or working with the band.

In a very competitive environment, publicity and promotion of the Artiste is paramount, to make the artiste stand out amongst the rest from other agencies, when out pitching for work.

The Artiste need to supply as much information as possible, together with publicity and photography materials to the Agency, so that the best and appropriate marketing effort by the Agency is employed to generate interest and secure work.

Questions have been raised about Artiste by passing the Client or being poached by the Client.

I find 98% of the Artiste on our book very loyal and would sometimes advised the Client to deal directly with us, when offered work by the Client.

Frank Forde, James Norton, Andy Keith and many more on Spectrum Agency book bless their hearts, have on many occasions been approached by the venues we booked them to appear, to see if they were prepared to be booked directly.

The standard reply were the usual straight and upright 'Call the Agency and they will do the bookings or one of the more humorous answer by a veteran singer was 'Call the agency, they are paying for my intercontinent pads.'

This is much appreciated and goes to show there are honourable men & women within the music circle. To reciprocate this loyalty and to recognize the good work of the Artistes, I would produce and display promotional materials, posters to be displayed at the venue where the Artiste is performing and deliver flyers door to door–minimum of a hundred to residents living in the surrounding estates of the venue.

Of course a concern to any agency is the possibility of the Artiste trying to get work directly from the pub/club. A clause in the Gig Confirmation contract states clearly to the parties that no work should be offered or sought at the same venue within a specific period.

It is a fair rule as time and effort have been put into the supplying and securing work to the venue and acts respectively.

Once a Gig is confirmed all Artistes will receive a Gig Confirmation providing full details of venue, time of the arrival, setup, sound check / performance time. Advice will also be given to safety aspects, parking and any other essential information.

An Agency has a responsibility to make sure the welfare & safety of each Artiste is look into in all venues played. I would usually recce a venue to ascertain stage area, loading area, and ensure that there is ample car park and that all health and safety issues are addressed. Very often, I would perform there with my band before sending any acts there.

Having first-hand information is always helpful especially so, when assigning work. The Artistes will generally be appreciative of this.

There have been occasions where pubs ask for a free performance and entice the band by saying if you are good, we will call you back.

If a band is starting out, perhaps but how would these pub landlord, who want something for nothing feel, if, they were told to go to somebody's house and cook a meal for their guests, free of charge, and if they like his cooking, then perhaps they will engage him for next party?

I am most fortunate to have worked with the majority of the artistes who have all been very professional in their attitude and work ethics. At the same time we have built a working relationship based on trust, friendship and goodwill and I have had the unexpected role of being a Counsellor and even babysitter.

There have been a number of occasions where I mediated between the Singers and their partners in disputes and offered advices and helped resolve personal issues.

On three occasions I was asked to babysit for a singing husband and wife team, so they could perform at a gig.

On certain times I have had calls from distressed artistes and had to offer some counselling over the phone, at 2 am in the early hour of the morning!

If it saves someone especially people you care about from any possible ugly outcome it is worth it!

Below are some real incidents that happened and how I dealt with the issues and resolved them-in the best way, possible or put in measures to stop it happening again in the near future.

Some thorny issues: Q & A

- **Artiste turning up late, no show, taken ill or performing not to standard and not to what has been agreed upon and expected.**

The audition and vetting of all Artistes from the very beginning is vital to ascertain the professional attitude and prior to engaging them is an important first step, to avoid such a situation developing.

I always maintain contact with all the Clients and Artistes up to their walking onto and off stage-thanks to the wonderful mobile phone. They can reach me anytime or leave a message and I would resolve any problems as best as possible in the circumstances.

- **Coming Late and Setting Up.**

There is no greater sin in live performance than arriving late at a venue. It will leave no time for the vital sound check and erode the confidence of the Client.

There were a few cases where the Landlord cancelled the gigs when the Artistes turned up late – between half an hour to 15 minutes before the time of performance.

He argued that the patrons who came earlier and waited in anticipation have all left for another pub, when there was no sign of the artiste setting up.

Patrons like to know and see that a live act is coming on.

I had to keep track on certain habitual late comers and advised them to better manage their time. I also had to impress on them the need to project a professional attitude and to consider the impact of their action in the cancellation of all future artistes by the venue.

- **Illness.**

In the unfortunate event of illness, keeping a list of the other Artistes on standby is useful should a replacement is needed at the last hour. For each Artiste the Agency send out, especially on important function, we always have someone ready to go at the last minute, should they be required.

- **Artiste by-passing agency and dealing directly with the Client.**

Any legal action for breach of contract should only be the last resort as it is time consuming, will destroy the goodwill built and may not have the desired result.

A handful have gone this way and even a Band that the agency recommended offered to play at nearly half of the fee for free drinks and a regular spot!

Ideal solution is best to not offer the acts anymore work and wish them well. Legal action is hardly worth it.

- **Not enough work for the Artiste.**

In very trying times in an Industry plagued with uncertainties, low patrons turnout and poor takings, I would normally give more consideration to the musician who is unemployed or facing harsh financial crisis by allocating solo work or even offering the singers work with a band, on the day they are not out working.

A few female Soloists works with my band on the occasion they have no work –this keeps them happy!

- **Bad behaviour, unprofessional attitude and bad stage antics and did not interact with the audience.**

This can be assessed earlier before sending any performer out so as to minimise any such behaviour and unprofessional attitude.
Below are some actual cases that the Agency experienced and some possible solutions:

Case A

There were Singers who would asked for advance pay from the landlord even before they started.

Asking for payment in advance by any artiste is not the right way unless there is prior agreement. It is not a standard practice-unless for big event, to ask for an advance for the usual pub gigs.

It will damage the Singer's reputation as well.

Case B

One even went to argue and confront cutomers who made a comment on her singing.

See possible solution as in Case C.

Case C

A fiery hot tempered Singer challenged a Customer to a fist fight over certain remarks.

An Artiste is there to entertain not to seek a fight.

The scene at a busy pub is normally noisy and patrons are boisterous and a few can be challenging.

Some are so drunk they hardly know their words and actions are out of order. This is where the Landlord should step in to remove them. It is not in the Artiste interest or role to respond aggressively to such people. It is tough restraining oneself in the face of provoked aggression or insults but Entertainers must accept it is part of the entertainment world.

There is always a clown, who will liven things up!

Unless someone become extremely aggressive or throw a punch, sometimes a little humour can damper a situation.

I once told a guy who was behaving like he has never seen a pretty girl and was harassing our young female singer, that if he continues to behave in such a disrespectful manner, I will phone his Mummy to come to take him home! He laughed almost non-stop and we managed to neutralised him-like Vet who neutered pets!

Case D

A Singer who is normally cool and collected lost it one particular hot night at a slightly tough pub full of football diehard fans of Manchester City.

He just packed his equipment and walked out just two minutes to going on stage.

His reasons being a fight broke out earlier and he was very afraid of his personal safety and especially worried about the possible damage to his guitar and equipment on stage, should another fight break out later.

In the above case, the Singer should have informed the pub of his concerns and acted more professionally instead of just packing up and walking out. He could have sought the help of the Landlord and get an assurance on the safety aspects both of his equipment and personal wellbeing.

Again one practical way is for the Landlord to remove the troublemakers. The Artiste could have laid down a condition that unless he got such assurance, he would have no choice but pack up and leave.

His abrupt action impacted upon the bookings of the other artistes, as the venue cancelled all the others, as soon as he stepped out of the door, that night. As I knew him personally and respected him for his past good work with the agency, I met up with him and listened to his side of the story.

Even though I do not agree with his action, I did impress upon him the loss of earnings for the rest of the Artistes, who had their bookings cancelled as a result of his walking out.

Luckily, the Agency did manage to find alternate work for them. I also did inform him that should this happen again the agency may have to review working with him.

Case E

Artiste totally refused to do a couple more songs after the encore, after the landlady accused her of taking the piss, when the demands by her customers went unheeded. It became an ugly situation resulting in the pub cancelling all the agency bookings.

Customers do take time to warm up and dance. By the time they do-Band is already into the last few numbers of the night. They are thinking of the nice long hot bath waiting for them at home-not the encore song!

Very often after playing the last song and especially when the crowd is really enjoying the performance, they would be clamoring for more, and perhaps more. Band members are exhausted at this stage.

A good idea is to tell the audience and prepare them that the band is wrapping up and will play the last few songs, for the evening. Slow numbers preferably.

Treat the two songs before encore number, as the last two and if the request comes in for more, then play out using the actual encore number.

Musicians should play on the last few numbers if there are request for it. This will keep the customers happy.

If they make a particular song request and if you are not able to play it well, then, offer an alternative song but never ignore the request. Perhaps when you return, you will offer to play that particular song for them?

In all the above incidents I had to speak to all sides to gather a fuller picture of the situation and try to find amicable solutions to satisfy all parties. Only by listening to all the parties involved, a possible way forward can be proposed.

The best approach to these problems is to foresee any issues and take steps to resolve them as well as to avoid coming to a point of no return.

- **Artiste did not receive full pay on the night of the performance.**

Again depending on the circumstances but if the venue don't feel they have got value for money, then, they may resort to trying, not to pay the full artiste fee.

The most appropriate action is to negotiate a reasonable fee happy to both sides. Generally, issue could be the Artiste was late, not engaging with the audience, not up to expectations and, in the worst scenario, drove customers away!

- **The Client stopped the Act and send Artiste home**

I have a 'Victor' test for new aritstes on the agency book. All new agency Acts are first sent to this small pub in Cheshire-kind of a guinea pig farm or a slaughterhouse for their very first 'live performance' If they are not good enough after their third song and if the audience complains, they are then sent packing, by the Landlord, Victor, who has a good ear for music.

If they survived 'the victor test', further bookings will follow. This Victor Test is the acid test.

In all fairness, I usually will send them to another pub in a different area and if a compliant follows, then it really was their last chance saloon moment.

- **Other Agencies poaching Artistes.**

There is really nothing to stop Artiste from moving to other agencies. In fact, it would be beastly and grossly unfair to do so. The best approach to minimize this happening is to build and harvest good working relationship with the artiste and to honour all commitments I have a friendly & professional relationship with all the Artistes in the Agency and very fortunately they treat me like a friend – in fact a few of them also stand in as Lead Singer, Bass player or drummer with my group, The Rhythm Jets.

- **Retirement of Artistes.**

As it is a people's business and age do catch up.

An agency to keep going would need to continue to seek out new & younger talents, so that it will have a steady pool of talents to replace anyone leaving or retiring.

- **Maintaining Goodwill**

It is vital to have a good working relationship with all the Artistes and the Clients – as there will be time when such goodwill based on trust and confidence is needed to overcome immediate or future problems.

A very common query from Clients seems to be the cost of hiring a singer/band and how I justify the costing.

- **What, it cost me £250 to hire a band for two forty-five minutes?**

I have often encountered prospective clients who would question the cost of engaging a performer.

'What the solo artiste cost me £150 and a band of four cost me £500 for 2 x45 mins set?'

'I could put on a karaoke for less than £80.'

That is a lot of money to pay for a performance of less than 2 hours they would suggest.

On the surface of it, it does appear so but if one look closely at all the time put into getting an act together, the fee is reasonable.

Most musicians are working at less than minimum pay per hour, if you take total hours involved in travelling to venue, setting up, performing and packing up.

I would then give them a breakdown of the actual cost of hiring a musician for the night it will appear as below:

- *The hours of practice by the musician*
- *The planning of the repertoire*
- *Insurance –personal & public liability*
- *Dress and presentation of the show*
- *Getting to the venue*
- *Setting up the equipment*
- *Sound check*
- *Getting ready and smartly dressed*
- *Short warm up in the changing room*
- *Performing to the agreed time*
- *Entertaining and looking confident & performing well and some play beyond the time booked, and if the crowd is up dancing in full force and demanding more*
- *Packing up*
- *Drained and driving home*

All Musicians would love to have a magic wand after a gig to pack away all the equipment.

If the total time is calculated from leaving home, setting up, sound checking, performing and packing up and right up to driving home, it would not be exaggerating to say, most musicians are working for a minimum wage or even below UK minimum wage, if all the hours are taken into account. Good Musicians do a good job and even have to smile in times of adversity!

Best things in life are free

Starting a business from zero and with a small capital is challenging and a learning curve and can be costly. But it don't need be costly if we scan around us the facilities and items that are available at a fraction of the actual cost or at a good discounted rate and even at no true cost at all. Yes, they can be free!

Office On Wheels

I started Spectrum Artiste Agency from my car equipped only with my mobile phone, a pen, a pocket size diary which I still use today and lots of prospects contact numbers plus a bottle of water which is often top up 'free' by the good staff of McDonalds in different town or area .

Going with a contract mobile broadband with free unlimited calls and free unlimited text is ideal if one is making lots of calls daily. I would normally make over a hundred calls per day till around midnight talking to musicians and landlords and managers of clubs and pubs.

Today there are business centres that offer the service of the new way of 'hot desking' where for a small daily, weekly or monthly fee, with flexible terms, one can come into an office and have a desk and other office support facilities. This is ideal for a start-up business wanting to keep the cost down and a space to do the necessary paperwork.

My car affectionately called 'Henry' is my office on wheels and operations centre.

I would normally park on free parking spaces in various locations, to make well over an hour of calls to prospects and artistes.

Why do people leave their engine running when they parked up to make calls? It's not only damaging the environment with carbon monoxide but also wasting petrol!

I have learned from past experience never park and sit in your vehicle near schools for long period of time, especially if it's an infant or primary school, to make calls. Expect the appearance of a police car if some highly alert and very civic minded member of the public to view your stationary car with you in dark glasses, as highly suspicious.

As my daily gigs hunting involves lots of driving in the beginning to introduce myself and also to cold call for work-the car, restaurants, KFC, McDonalds, cafes and public libraries serve as 'free' office space to do the administration work.

Over a cup of coffee I would usually record the prospects visited and pour over the details and do some follow up calls.

For budding musicians there are many useful websites to search for fellow musicians or join a band:

www.partysounds.co.uk
www.bandmix.co.uk
www.musicians-in-the-city.co.uk
www.gumtree.co.uk
www.loot.co.uk

Have you ever wondered what the missing chord or the lyrics to a song is?

Wonder no more, as help is just a click away!

Pressto! Or 'Press the keys' on and look up:

www.ultimate-guitar.com
www.guitartab.com
www.911tabs.com
www.dotmusic.com
www.metrolyrics,com
www.lyrisfreak.com
www.chordie.com

A lot of musicians I know are broke, most of the time.

So if you need free things, do check up on the net and for free furniture see:

www.money.co.uk,
www.wasteonline.org.uk,
www.thecloud.net

For free clothes and food, there are certain charities that provide free emergency accommodation and some run soup kitchen where you can get free hot meals and drinks.

The free wi-fi service at certain outlets, and the free internet usage at public libraries, with photocopy, fax and printing facilities, certainly help to speed up the correspondence with the Artistes, the Clients and all the Musicians.

It will certainly contribute to the increase in turnover of the agency business.

Free wi-fi & use of table space at eateries for paper work and mobile calls. All for a cup of coffee-but observe the time limit for parking.

Free use of outdoor space especially on a lovely sunny day!

Free street park & call …. and free use of pub or public library facilities & free heating.

Free use of Client's premise after putting up the posters and courtesy call.

Other Freebies in Life
Advice, Hugs, Kisses, Smiles & Fresh Air

Getting It Going

Getting Ready

'What, you mean it will cost me £150 to pay a Singer to do two spots of 45 minutes set? 'Isn't that a bit too much to pay someone to stand there and sing, what is actually like karaoke, for one and a half hour.' A bewildered pub landlord exclaimed on hearing the rate for engaging an artiste.

'I can get a customer to do it for a pint of beer and some peanuts' he protested.

I pointed out the Artiste is no karaoke singer.

He or she is an Entertainer and Singer. They have been practicing and polishing up their acts and presentation so that they can stand and deliver an evening of good entertainment tailored to the kind of audience expected at the event.

The hours of hard work that goes into their repertoire and their stage antics will be their testimony and will reflect on how well they will be received by the patrons.

Getting ready will mean preparing the list of songs and knowing the age and type of patrons and the event itself. The Artiste or Band may have to learn certain new songs and know the lyrics well and cater to any special song request for that special occasion.

If it's a wedding, discussion will need to be held with the Bride & Groom to select the songs of their choice especially the happy couple chosen 'Dance number'

On occasion such as weddings, appropriate titles are very important. Imagine the looks on all the guests if the singer were to sing 'Please release me let me go …by Engelbert Humperdinck.'

'These boots are made for walking' is another no no.

Then there is the stage clothes. If it's Halloween, it's all the scary outfits.

Most bands and performers in England & elsewhere in the U.K.

generally wear casual & comfortable clothes when performing at pubs but clubs demand a more formal dressing.

If one takes into account the hour of practice and the preparation, the travelling, the setting up of the equipment and sound check and the performance the £150 paid to a Solo Singer or the £250 to a band is well worth it! On average an Artiste will have to spend up to eight hours per gig, that is from leaving home, performing on stage and getting home. Not to forget that he or she has to keep on smiling and being entertaining whilst on stage!

Getting There

If you are thinking of venturing into the world of music entertainment and would like to be on stage making waves (making other people happy!) the first thing you will need to do after sorting out your repertoire and having an idea of your type of audience is to have transport to get there.

I know of musicians using taxis. Unless your Uncle is a taxi driver or your boyfriend or girlfriend can drive you, hailing taxis can be mighty expensive.

Mario from my favourite country, Italy, one of the drummers who plays in Rhythm Jets the covers function group, actually and

practically carry his drum kit in two handy bags onto buses and trains to gigs. Mama mia!

It only cost a Fiver!
Mario with his mini x'mas drums kit from Papa in Italy

Do give yourself ample time to get to the venue and have a mental picture of the destination by checking out the direction on the internet, satnav or map. A speeding fine will wipe out your earnings. If all else fails just head to the town of the venue and try asking the locals.

Getting It Going

The all essential sound check before the start of any performance is so vital. To ignore this part would be madness and the sound quality could turn out badly. It is always a good idea to turn up early (an hour and a half before actual showtime) to set up sound check and discuss the set list and have a have a general feel of the venue.

In clubs, there is the customary changing room where Artistes change into their stage outfits and it is like a holding area before they step into the limelight. It's quite exciting really!

Getting Applause

Musicians feed off the applause of the audience. It's like a tonic and without it, the atmosphere can be pretty dull and down, even to the point of being a sleepy kind of feeling for the performers!

On stage, one has to deliver. The patrons are there to be entertained and to get their applause the Act has to look and sound good in every way. Polished & well-presented and engaging is the word. No one want to see a miserable, unhappy or unenthusiastic face on stage.

They have enough problems of their own already, before coming to watch some entertainment for relaxation and chilling out. It will bore them to death to see Entertainers –unentertaining, uncomfortable and totally miserable!

The applause, according to an old Chinese proverb is like the oil that keeps the engine going. It drives the Artiste to perform and deliver with gusto! It's the reward for performing well, a big pat on the back for musicians.

It's nothing more disheartening then to play to an empty room or an unappreciative crowd.

So when a performance has gone well and crowd get up to dance and ask for more, you know you have done a good job. The only problem here is, when they only start to warm up and dance when the band is playing their last two numbers and want another half hour of music.

Usually the band will oblige and do an encore and play without charge if it is only the extra two or three songs.

An understanding pub landlord would offer additional fee if the band was requested to play say, half an hour.

The encore is the yardstick and benchmark of any Artiste or Band.

Getting Offstage

Generally the majority of Bands & Artistes follow the standard 2 x45 minutes set and very often the patrons would ask for an encore.

The encore is the accolade to the Entertainer –the topping of the cream so to speak. It's the yardstick that signify that the evening performance has been a success and the audience have been truly entertained and want more!

Staying and performing an extra two or three songs for the encore will reasonably be enough to satisfy the patrons but musicians have been known to play for longer-sometimes at the offer of extra pay.

Very often when the party goers are enjoying the music and band, they keep demanding another and another last song.

It can go on all night, if the crowd is not prepared for the ending of the performance.

Playing more than an hour into the second set, it can be tiring and exhausting for the members of the group.

One trick I used, is to announce before the last three songs of the final set 'Thank you so much everyone, you have been a lovely audience, we like to take you home but we can't, so let us all get on the dance floor to our last two numbers before we say adios and goodnight'

So the band was actually playing the last two songs before the encore numbers. And sure as night follows day, after the last two numbers, the shout of 'more' will come and that will mean playing the arranged encore numbers as planned.

It's good to get offstage when the timing is right.

Getting Paid

Musicians like getting paid in hard cold cash for practical reasons. Most musicians I know are hard strapped for money for those whose only income is the weekend gigs and they rely solely on that to survive.

Some establishments insist on paying in cheques either on the night itself or in a couple of weeks, after submitting to their Head Office. Whatever the agreed arrangements it has to be a comfortable one for all.

Getting Rebooking

The best gift and sweet music to any musician is to get a rebooking. It says a lot, for it spells out clearly the response to their act. One is tempted to ask for more 'dole' 'dosh' 'bread' and international 'cash' in musician language depending which part of the UK you are in, but it would be better to quote an increase in fee after a couple more gigs at the same venue.

Gently easing in and gaining the confidence of the pub/club are the key words.

Getting Home

Packing up is the bane of all musicians, wires here, wires there, wires everywhere and dismantling all the equipment can be tedious especially all you want to do is get paid and get home-soon. Most musicians would love to have a magic wand and make all the gear packed up and disappear with a wave!

Driving home after a gig is the best feeling especially with money in your pocket and a smile on your face, knowing you gave a good performance and all those hours of hard work rehearsing and fine tuning your act has been well received by the audience.

Getting Laid

The best part after a gig is getting laid. Lying in a warm long bath filled with bubbly fragrant bubble bath and listening to a rendition by Andrea Bocelli is just pure heaven!

Getting Good Sleep

Most musicians find it difficult to go to bed to have a nice sleep after an adrenalin pumping gig. They need to relax and unwind when they arrive home all very exhausted. I find listening to classical and smooth jazz music a great way to relax and a glass of wine can help one on the way to counting sheep. I was told very recently to my total surprise that in the English language, more than one sheep is still written and pronounced as sheep. Eh? How can this be?

I have been sending texts to English friends for years wishing them a good kip 'Goodnight and happy counting sheeps'

No wonder some have told me they could not sleep after my text sent at 1am in the morning!

I am beginning to suspect, it may be my spelling and the saying 'sheeps' instead of 'sheep' ?

I am still puzzled, as one goat and two goats, one pig and two pigs, one dog and two dogs, one jag and two jags. One sheep and two sheep? Confused? English is fun!

Quick checklist before you leave home for the gig:

Phone venue a day or a week ahead to make all ok. All gig quipment, plectrums, extra guitar, leads, strings are on board and are in good condition

- » The Set List
- » Your stage clothing
- » You had a good meal
- » You had a good adequate rest
- » Car in good condition-tyres, water, oil level
- » De-icer, scraper, shovel, gloves, warm clothing, thermos hot flask, torchlight, snacks for winter breakdown.

- » Enough fuel in car
- » Sat-nav & address of venue
- » Breakdown Cover
- » Mobile phone charged fully
- » Money
- » Hugs & Kisses from loved ones
- » *Finally…..don't forget to bring yourself!*

One more tip

- » On Arrival –Setting Up /Sound Check
- » Check area allocated for performance.
- » If there are any difficulties, refer to the Manager to clear the area.

Health and Safety –Wirings & Band Area

Ensure all wirings from main plugs running along the floor to PA System are safely taped down.

When people are dancing near the artiste / band, they get caught up in the party mood.Due care must be taken to prevent injury to anyone ,who may accidentally knock the speakers over or trip on some wirings.

Extra care must be taken if there are young children around the stage area. Politely request that they stay away from the huge speakers and main stage.

Sound Check

The essential sound check to get the right balance and sound. No Artiste or Band should ignore this very important step, prior to starting the performance.

How to speak English Chinese style!

When I first landed on British soil, almost all the English look alike to me. The British seem to think that too, of the Chinese people especially when we all have black colour hair.

Many years later now, I can tell the difference a little bit better but still struggle with the different regional accents.

Mixing with the local native English, I have noticed that they too struggle to understand the accents of their own people and foreigners like the Chinese. Working with Musicians in the music circle and kids in English Schools there are numerous funny occasions where certain words are misunderstood.

The Chinese struggle to pronounce English words especially when the language is not their first and words and sentences with the alphabets

'R' and 'L' comes out the reverse.

'R' is pronounced as 'L' as in Row becomes Low and 'Lucky' is 'Rucky'

To illustrate some examples I have listed below the English to Chinese pronunciation and how a Chinese tongue would see and pronounce the R & L in communicating with English people.

- » Arrive- Alive *What time did you aLive today ?*
- » Allow- ARow *Can you aRow me in ?*
- » Aeroplane - AeLowpRane
- » Bread-BLead
- » Blue-Brue Brue CoRoul
- » Bloom-Broom
- » Bring-BLing *Can you bling some cash ?*

- » Brown-BLown
- » Diplomacy-DipRomacy
- » Develop-DeveRope-
- » Envelope –EnveRope
- » England- EngRand
- » Fly- Fry *I fry to Hong Kong Tomorrow*
- » Free-Flee- *Are You Flee tomolow?*
- » Friend- Fliend *Nikki is my new Fliend*
- » Laugh-Raugh
- » Lazy-Racy
- » Look- Rook
- » Love- Rove *Rove me tender*
- » Lovely- Rougly *Have a Roughly birthday*
- » Little- Ritter
- » Low- Row
- » Political –Prolitical
- » Police- PRoReece *PRoReece Stration.*
- » Please- PRease *Prease help me*
- » Proud- Ploud *PLoud Maly*
- » Radio-Laydio
- » Rice-Lice *Would you like some FlyLice ?*
- » River –Liver
- » Road-Load
- » Ready -Laydy *Are you Ready Are you Lady ?*
- » Rover-Lover *Rover has become the Lover*
- » Rough- Love

- » Spring- Spling Have some spling loll
- » Suddenly-SundenRy Sudenry he came
- » Sugar-Suega
- » Swallow-SawRRoe
- » Teddy-TeRRy
- » Time- TRime
- » Ticket-TRicket *TRicket To Lide*
- » Tramp-Telamp
- » Television- TeRRevision
- » Tomorrow- TomoLLow
- » Temporary- TempoLaly It is only tempoLaly.
- » Umbrella-Umbella
- » Underground-UndReGLound
- » United- Unitred
- » Very- VeLy
- » Velvet-VelRet
- » Wonderful-WonDREful Oh how wondREful
- » Wrong-Wong
- » Wally-WaRRY
- » Yellow-YeRROw *YeRRow submaLine*

When Mao Met Nixon

The Orientals can get the English words all twisted up sometimes – all Wok and Roll up as they sprinkle 'Sore finger' (I learned this from the pupils in schools, that every time they ask for salt & vinegar, their local chippy, Chinese chap will parrot phrase 'you want sore finger?') on the English plate of Fish & Chips.

Sore finger on your fish & chips? I don't think so!

Here's a joke told by a friend concerning the Legendary Revolutionary Communist Party Chinese Leader, the Old Soldier and Chairman Mao Tse Tung of China, who hardly ever spoke English.

In preparing for the first official visit by an American President Richard Nixon, the Chinese leader, Chairman Mao began practicing his poor command of the English Language with the aid of a Tutor, six months before the President's arrival. History records it as the week that changed the world.

Every day for the past months, Chairman Mao would pace up and down reciting the greetings sentence 'Hello, Mr. President, several times over and over and How are you? and repeating this several times every three hour interval.

Hello Mr. President, how are you?

Hello Mr. President, how are you?

Hello Mr. President, how are you?

After a few months Chairman excitedly proclaimed to his English tutor.

'I think I got it, Yes, I think I got it' exclaimed a delighted Chairman Mao to the delight of his English Tutor.

On the day of Nixon's arrival, Chairman Mao while waiting for the President's Air Force One to land kept repeating in his head what he had learned and repeated the ' Hello Mr. President, how are you? 'Hello, Mr President, how are you mantra.

Eventually the plane came to a halt near the red carpet, specially laid out on the tarmac, the door flung opened, and out step President Nixon and his wife.

Standing ready to greet Nixon, the Chairman Mao was confident and ready to show off his newly learned English greetings and words of hospitality to President Nixon.

As the President approached him, Chairman Mao smiled but got a bit nervous as he shook Nixon's hand and greeted him with the following:

'Harro Mr. President, Welcome to the Peoples RepuBRICK of China, Who are you?

Gan Pei 乾杯
(A Chinese greeting for "Bottoms up!")

A Chinese man and an English man were dining in a restaurant.

The Chinese man lifted his glass up and made a toast to the English man, "Gan Pei" (Cheers). The English man was confused but he continued eating.

This happened a few times and whenever the Chinese man wanted to drink he would always say "Gan Pei"

The English man only nodded and silently continued to drink and eat.

Not long after, the Chinese man once again said, "Gan Pei" whilst lifting up his glass.

This time, the English man put down his cutlery and angrily said to the Chinese man,

"It's all right if you CAN'T PAY!" I'll pay!
So just shut up."

When eat all you can does NOT mean ALL you can and ALL DAY long!

A Chinese Restaurant put up this sign to deter customers from overstaying.

Wok & Roll

Lost in translation

- That's not right — Sum Ting Wong
- You harbouring a fugitive? — Hu Yu Hai Ding
- See me as soon as possible — Kum Hai Nao
- Stupid Man — Dum Fuk
- Small Horse — Tai Ni Po Ni
- Did you go to the beach — Wai You So Tan?
- I bumped into a coffee table — Ai Bang Mai Fa Kin Ni
- I think you need a face lift — Why So Dim?
- Are you on diet? — Wai You Mun Ching?
- This is a tow away zone — No Pah King
- Meeting next week — Wai You Kum Nao?
- Staying out of sight — Lai Ying Lo
- What do you think — Wok Yew Ting
- Why are you late? Wai Yew Leck
- Who said that? Woo Say Tat
- Who Fart ? Hoo Fatt
- Need rest, can't work — Goh Sik Dong
- Salt & Vinegar — Sore Finger
- I can do it — Soo Kan Ai
- Put Kettle On — Yu Wan Ti
- Let's go to the movie — See Pik Tar

- » A Pickpocket — Han Goh Far
- » I am in charge, How Can I Help ? — Hoo Yin Char
- » How many did he get? — Yee Gok Wan
- » He has received it — Hee Gok Yik
- » You must be kidding — Hai Ho Low
- » You are having a laugh — Soo Man Fun
- » Who's on the line? — Hoo Onn Liang
- » Do you have passport? — Shoo Mee Chop
- » What shoes size? — Wok Choo Sai
- » Where are you going? — Soh Goh Wei
- » Excellent — Far Kin Goot
- » Bad Day — Low Dong Dei
- » Bad Hair Day — Nu Lok Goot

Allreet Now & Jolly Good !
English as spoken by some Northerners

For the benefit of Singaporeans, Malaysians and Visitors from the Far East who plan to visit the North of England a knowledge of the following slang words and phrases spoken by the Northerners and their meaning can be helpful .

I have based this on my experience in North West of England as a Supply Teacher in British Secondary Schools and through interaction with the locals and with fellow musicians. Though it's not comprehensive it will represent and give an idea on how these words and expressions are used in daily conversation with the local natives.

In North England, they call men' blokes' and women 'birds'

Some local phrases by the North Native English, I have come across:

Aw......sounds like the word 'Or' The British say this to empathise, say with a sad story or they see something cute, they go ' aw ! aw! that is cute.

- » As well - Also
- » Any road – Anyway
- » Alright Cock? – how are you ? Sometimes come across as Alreet Cock? Nothing to do with the male anatomy. It is an old English greeting
- » Alreet Love?-how are you in a more friendly and familiar way
- » You Alreett? -Are you well? –a common daily greetings exchanged between the Northern English.
- » You what- What do you mean?
- » What's to do? -Hey, what happening?
- » Me dad or Me Mum - My father or My Mother.

- Summat to eat- Getting something to eat (mainly in Lancashire)
- Put wood in hole- lock the door (a very old English saying used in certain part of Lancashire)
- My Mate or Me Mate - My Friend.
- Don't like Gum - Don't Like them (nothing to do with chewing gum)
- Sound - good
- It's sound mate – used by Liverpool people to mean ' it's good my friend'
- Brill or Ace - brilliant or awesome. In Liverpool they say it is 'Ace'
- Aggro - trouble. 'He is giving me a lot of aggro.'
- Ops se daisy- Oh my goodness
- Okie dokie - alright or everything is fine with me
- You What? - What do you mean?
- Friggin - Can be a rude word depend on the way of the expression. mean F...
- You will get done -You will be fined or punished by the law
- Yee buy Gum- Again nothing to do with asking you to go and buy chewing gum but a Yorkshire accent to mean ' Oh dear'
- Bloody Murder -An angry Englishman way of letting off steam.
- It's shite - It's not good –in fact terrible or smell disgusting
- Do me head in- You are messing me up or confusing me.
- Stop miderring me - Don't disturb me, I'm thinking
- AAAAA..............normally a Liverpool (Liverpudlian) will start a sentence in this manner.
- Get off me- Go away
- Don't be daft - Don't be silly

- » Ain't it? - Is it not?
- » Bender- heavy drinking session or going from pub to pub drinking
- » Bloody - Common swear word used as an expression of surprise. Mostly expressed as 'bloody hell' or 'bloody awful'
- » Bob's your uncle - That is how you do it
- » Bog - Toilet
- » Bodge- to do a bad task
- » Bollocks – English use this word when they are angry or think some issue or thing is a 'load of rubbish' or unbelievable
- » Bugger All- Cheap or cost nothing at all
- » Bleeding – bloody
- » Calling Him/ Her - Talking bad about her/him
- » Carrying On - Having an affair. 'He is carrying on with his next door neighbour' Nothing to do with helping the neighbour with carrying her Tesco shopping bags
- » Cheers or Cheerio – Goodbye
- » Clear off – Go away (Fast!)
- » Chuffed to bits – happy feeling
- » Cock up – mess up
- » Codswallop –like making up a story or lie
- » Crap - Bad
- » Daft - Silly 'Don't be daft'
- » Donkey's years- Many years have passed 'I have not seen you for donkey's years
- » Fancy – Like. 'Do you fancy going to the park?'
- » Fanny- It refers to the female vagina. In the Far East especially in Malaysia, Thailand & Singapore there are women using this name, without realising it is a rude word. There is an erotic

book title 'Fanny Hill'

- Fit- in England normally refers to a person. 'God, she is fit' to mean she is very adequate.
- Flog it – Sell it
- Flutter- Have a bet
- Full of Beans - Full of Energy
- Gagging for it – Not a nice word with sexual attachment. Never ever say to any English Girl that you or her is gagging for it. You will get a nice tight slap and possibly end up in court-unless she is your girlfriend or partner.
- Get Stuffed – Get lost, Go away
- Give us a bell - Phone or contact me
- Gobsmacked - Pleasantly surprised
- Gutted – Feeling down, Disappointed
- Hard – Tough with some fighting spirit. Hear this a lot in Schools among the kids. 'He is hard'
- Honest to God – I swear by the God, it is the Truth
- Hunky Dory - No worries , all OK
- Jammy- Lucky
- Jolly - Excellent.
- Kip – Short rest
- Knackered - Tired. Sounds like 'naked'. If the English chap (bloke) says he is knackered ,it does not mean he going take out his trousers. Don't worry he is too tired anyway, to do anything else but to rest & go to sleep
- Knees up – To have a celebration - chatting, drinking & dancing. The British sure like to party especially weekends
- Knockers – Breasts .Usually refer to female parts not door knockers.

- Leg it – Run away
- Made up – happy and a sense of contentment
- Mint- Good
- Meither – To pester
- Mug - Silly. He is a mug means he is a silly person or gullible
- Naff - Not cool
- Naff Off - Get Lost
- Nancy – Soft
- Next door but one - the house after the next one
- Nice One – Well done
- Nick it – To Steal.
- Nookie - Doing something naughty
- Not My Cup of Tea - Not to my taste
- Nowt – Nothing
- Off Your Trolley – Crazy
- On the piss – To go out drinking till drunk
- On about – What are you on about means what are you talking about?
- On your bike - Get lost please, in a polite way
- Owt – Anything
- Piece of Cake – It is easy
- Porkies - Lies
- Posh – High Class
- Prat – Silly
- Pull A Bird or Bloke – chat up and secure a date with girl or boy
- Pillock - Much ruder than prat
- Puff – Gay

- Queer – Can mean gay or ill
- Quid - British pound
- Shirty – Being bad tempered
- Skiving – To avoid work
- Slapper – A loose woman
- Tart – Cheap, If refer to woman, it is not very nice nor complimentary but degrading. Can also mean a pastry like egg tart
- Slag off - To bad mouth
- Smashing – Very Good, Fantastic or Terrific
- Snog – Serious kissing
- Sod –Many meanings and uses. Sod it means leave it.
- Sorted – Solved
- Stuff it – Can't be bothered with something. 'Who cares! Stuff It'
- Taking The Mickey – Making fun of
- Ta- Thanks
- Taking the biscuits - To out do
- Taking The piss – To make a joke of someone
- Tosser – see Wanker
- Twit - Idiot
- Wacky backy – kind of drugs/ weed
- Wanker – same as Tosser
- Well up – tears
- Wind up - tease
- Wonky - shaky
- Ta – Thanks

- The natives have also shorten certain words in their daily conversation. Below are some examples :
- Gonna - Going to
- Wanna - Want to
- Gotta - Got to ….I have got to get a message to you would be said as… 'Gotta get a message to you'
- Hafta – Have to
- Coulda - Could have
- Shoulda - Should have
- Woulda - Would have
- Musta - Must have
- Lotsa - a Lot of something –Lots of money
- Sorta - sort of or kind of or a little bit
- Sick – really awesome or very good. English slang it means cool
- Wicked - awesome
- Are you taking the mickey out of me? - Are you trying to be funny
- Take the piss – making fun of someone
- I'm pissed – I'm drunk
- It's pissing down heavy - It's raining heavy
- Nought - nothing
- How some Northern Lancashire people pronounce certain common words. The letter T is emphasised.
- Dad - Dart
- Mum - Momb
- Flour - Flower
- Advertisement - AdverTISEment

- » Birmingham - Birming GUM
- » Oldham - OldTHEM and not pronounce as OldHAM
- » Nottingham – NottinGUM, not NottingHAM
- » Love - Loaf
- » Tonight - Toneet
- » It – Hit
- » Hospital - 'Ospital
- » Hope - 'Ope
- » Up - Oop
- » Occasion - H'occasion
- » Money – Mor nay
- » Butter - Bot'ah
- » Britain - Brig'in
- » Letter – Let-'Ah
- » Bus – Boost
- » Help - 'Elp
- » Pub – Poop

Whenever I phone pubs looking for work, I would say I wish to speak to the pup landlord. As in PUP, to the amusement of the person at the end of the line. Some just put the phone down! I realised later I should have said and pronounced 'pup' as POOP! to get a better response.

Not so nice words Used by some natives

& Fun With English Words

- » Bog – Toilet.
- » Bullocks – Testicles.
- » Bugger off – go off, if the English say this to you it mean they want you to leave.
- » Piss Off (Low medium volume) - Go away!
- » Piss Off! (Loud angry volume) - Run away fast from the English Guy!
- » Get the F... out of here! (Low medium volume) – Go away soon.
- » Get the F... out of here now!! (Loud angry volume) - Run away fast! Don't argue.
- » Wanker - A person who spend a lot of time by himself and is a very handy person.
- » Two finger sign with inner palm facing you is a way to say go away – not to be confused with V Victory sign which is a peace sign, with palm facing outwardly.
- » Twat - Check the English Dictionary, it has something to do with the female anatomy but used on male population in England. (a vulgar word for vulva and an insulting term meaning a weak or contemptuous individuals).Not very complimentary, if the English call you this. If they call you this, just tell them 'You Know Nothing' This will usually work or annoy them. The very fact that you don't know the meaning of this word will irritate and frustrate them more and they will leave you alone. Next when they look at you slightly puzzled,

look into their eyes and tell them to, Piss Off!

- » This can usually work.
- » There is a place in the Shetland Island by this expletive name called Piss.
- » Piss – urinate.
- » Pissing down - It's raining heavy.
- » Shiat - The human waste- they use it to mean it is deplorable or terrible.
- » Nobhead - Someone the English refer to as not so stable or having a wobbling head.
- » Speak with fork tongue – telling different versions.
- » I am shagged - The British have different meaning for this word depending how and when it is used. If he is worn down from work he would say 'I am shagged'. Otherwise it can have a sexual connotation-refering to their bedroom conquest or adventures.
- » Dickhead - Combining Nobhead and Wanker. Not a nice complimentary term.
- » Plonker - Quite similar to above description of nobhead.
- » Queer - A Gay person
- » Thick -Not so smart or stupid.
- » Chav- not a bright person or same as thick.
- » Frigin around - wasting time.
- » Spend a penny - go to the bathroom.
- » Tally Ho - used in fox hunting, shouted when a rider or follower sees the fox. Sort of an alarm call to go into action.
- » Telling porkies – telling lies
- » A lot of shite – A load of rubbish

The English Language can be fun !

Nouns on the Run
Words absconding from the page.

Nans on the Run
Mass escape from care home

Buns on the Run
Breakout from cake shop.

Nuns on the Rum
Mother superior will be absolutely furious !

Huns on the Run
Attila and his army are beaten.

Nuns on the Run
Convent outing to remains of old abbey

Cows on The Run
No Milk Today

Band on the Run- *Paul McCartney on Tour*

A Signed Copy from a Beatle!

Yes, I need to shout out LOUD! My prized possession signed autograph from Sir Paul McCartney sent to me from his London Office in1993, when I was back home.

I really did not expect a reply after a friend challenged me to get a signed autograph from him. All I wrote on an envelope was:

To Sir Paul McCartney, Beatles Somewhere on a hill in Southern England.

I was shocked it was received by his office in London and equally surprised to get a signed postcard in return!

More Fun with the English Language - Eunonym

- » A Eunonym is a name that seems to fit its bearer perfectly (aptronyn)
- » Sara Blizzard - BBC Weather Reporter
- » Russell Brain – Neurologist
- » Usain Bolt – 100 m-200m Gold Medallist
- » Margaret Court –Tennis Player
- » Bob Rock - Music Producer
- » Alto Read - Sax Player
- » Tim Armstrong – Wrestler
- » Mike Cook - Chef
- » Andrew Law - Solicitor
- » Connie Tan – Tanning Salon Operator
- » Richard Bird – Pet Shop Owner
- » Ghitar Patel – Guitar Store Staff
- » Colin Bell – Alarm Bell Salesman
- » May Lai - Beds Saleswoman
- » Toby Cash - Bank Staff

Mix & Match

It has been and still is, a wonderful experience to play with different Musicians of different musical genre.

Ever wondered why Musicians all over the world use the expression 'play' and not 'work' when referring to their performing on stage.

'I was playing at the birthday party last night'

'The band played at the Conservative Club last night.'

Strangely and contagiously this expression has spread to non-musicians as well, almost universally.

My friends and relatives, some with no knowledge of the music world, would enquire

'Are you playing tonight?' or 'Where are you playing next Sunday?'

I suppose to most musicians, they don't work in a 9-5pm situation. They see their music playing as an art and a labour of love and not like 'work'. in the true sense.

It's quite funny when someone ask 'Are you playing with Madeline tonight? Or 'Did you play with Angie last week?' The question has a sensual or even suggestive naughtiness about it. Or 'Is Carol playing with you this coming Saturday?

It can hilarious and sound so funny at times!

It would not be so funny if a Mechanic was asked this same question instead of directed to a musician.

Consider the reaction of the wife of the Mechanic if she were to overhear such a question directed to her husband

Imagine this real conversation related to me by a drummer.

'Last Sunday, I was playing and backing Julie at the Social Club'

Really? I asked.

Did the audience enjoyed what they heard and saw? I enquired.

Yes, it was heaving and I was banging away, Julie and I were exhausted at the end of the evening.

They kept wanting more! replied the drummer.

What did you do next ? I press on- I was curious.

So we did 'Hold On I'm Coming for the climax' ha ha, said the drummer.

With a Little help from my friends

In the past, the band I was in used to turn down work for various reasons but one of the reasons I thought should be addressed is the unavailable service of the bass player or drummer

There have been numerous occasions where the Bass player or drummer is not available and we just let work pass us by.

Thinking of a way to solve this, I started to seek out Musicians who were seeking bands that were seeking players for the odd gig.

The key to filling in the gap is to phone a friend. It has been a marvellous opportunity to work (play) with so many talented musicians in the UK.

It has indeed been a privilege to perform with different drummers, bassists, keyboardists, guitarist and vocalists.

A journey of sharing ideas and improving playing standards in our respective instruments.

Starting to contact suitable replacements which were recommended by fellow musician friends and through searching online on the net, the list is expanding and growing.

Today I work with a talent pool of:
30 drummers,
20 Bassists,
20 lead vocalists,
10 Keyboardists
50 Guitarist /Vocalists
5 saxophonists
8 percussionists
5 violinists.

The best part of it is, almost all have become friends and there is a happy bond of friendship, trust and good chemistry among us.

Tapping from this pool of talent, I put together Rhythm Jets, a band of experienced Musicians.

Mix & Match

To make life easy for all –I apply the Standard & an almost Common Set List for all musicians debbing with the band.

I have put together a band in less than an hour, and in the next couple of hour or weeks, the band is on stage playing like they have been together for years!

This is made possible by putting a simple plan in place.

I like to refer it to as the 'Band-In-An-Hour' Plan or 'Band Hour' plan. The Plan is to assemble the right Musicians for the right gig, all in an hour by contacting them via email and mobile phone.

Once again, the wonderful electronic world of today transmit instant messages and replies in a flash! Let your fingers do the walking.

To start off, it's vital that at least two members of the band know exactly what they are doing, how the songs flow, so that the others in the group will find it easier to follow. Essentially, there must be an understanding by the members of the band, especially the two core members, of the structure of the song - the start, the middle and the ending.

I start off the 'Band Hour' plan by calling to find out who is available for a 4 piece group or a particular date.

Then the next step is arranging a practice with the bass player and later a practice with the singer over the phone or at a convenient place (Pubs are usually quiet in the afternoon and a little corner would suffice) with an acoustic guitar and the voice and at a further later stage, talk about the repertoire over the phone with the Drummer.

Once all the members have been through each number of the Set List and are comfortable to go with it, the next step is one full band rehearsal before the gig date.

From past experience, bands that practice for a long time without playing any gigs tend to break up.

I came to know of a group that practice until perfect each note and lyrics at almost every weekend but broke up without playing a single gig!

Though practice does indeed makes perfect, mental preparation and practice over the phone is almost but not totally, just as good.

In discussing the set list with the Singer, it is a good idea to run through each song over the phone and make a mental note of the flow of the song, taking into account the instrumental and harmony parts.

There have been occasions where I have put together musicians who have not met each other and we all turn up at the gig introducing ourselves, to the amusement of the patrons and Landlord. As long as the Band play and entertain well, the pub will appreciate it.

I always advise Musicians not to let the pub or club know that the band was put together just a couple of hours or weeks ago,

From a couple of experiences, some pubs try not to pay the full amount when they find out the band was meshed together, for the one gig, even though all the members are experienced musicians.

The telling sign will be when the group start to discuss what song to play next. To avoid this situation developing, all members are sent set list ahead of the gig and discussed over the phone.

My ingredients for a Good Mixed Band:

- » *Select from a wide pool of musicians*
- » *Check availability*
- » *Choose the right mix of musicians to suit the occasion*
- » *Put in a good selection of mixed repertoire of song from a wide genre of music*
- » *Mixed it with group of experienced players*
- » *The Musicians check out and practise their parts*
- » *The Musician (at least two) come together to practise the Set,*
- » *Stir up the combination and shake it all over in a 'jar'*
- » *Hey presto!, pour out the content.*

Hopefully the result will be a rich and new and good combination of varied taste, sometime exotic and a vast pool of talent and great musicianship combined with an interesting new sound.

Getting together different musicians of varied background, with different personalities, to come to work together, and assembling them in one place to practise, especially if the band is a twelve piece, can be quite challenging.

It's always sad to hear that some bands practise for hours on end only to break up, even before doing one single gig or after a handful.

Sensing this and not wanting to let gigs go by (which I did in the past),putting a band of musicians who are in different bands together for a certain gig and event seem like a good workable idea.

At least this type of 'free & easy ' or 'pay as you go ' or 'scratch' band cannot break up!

It's only good if all learn their parts, otherwise it will end up like a jam session especially when the musicians have never played together previously nor even met each other.

The wonderful world of internet, mobile and the old faithful telephone all help to make it work, even if the drummer, bassist, guitarist and vocalist all live hundreds of miles apart or even overseas.

Over the years, I have built up an extensive network of musicians from all background all over the UK and Europe.

The Rhythm Jets, the group I put together with different lead vocalists-both male and female, bassists, keyboardists, guitarists and drummers have played over a thousand gigs in the North West & other parts of England.

The magic of 'YouTube' web page provide an excellent resource and a station where musicians can stopover, visit and check out the song in mind and work out the structure and chords of the tune.

The next step is to have a practise with all the members, or if not, at least one core member of the Band. This creates a foundation for the repertoire.

There are a couple of video clips of the 'scratch band 'or 'get four musicians unknown to each other and see what happen' band on YouTube.

Key in 'The Rhythm Jets' on the channel and see the video clips of the band on YouTube.

First Impression is everything!

It is often said one will never get a second chance, if first impression fails. How very true! No amount of good excuses will change the initial poor impression, if it was badly delivered in some form or manner.

I try to impress upon the 'last minute, put together' band members to play and perform like we have been together for years. Indeed at some functions, we get remarks like 'The band is great! 'That was a brilliant set, how long have you all been together? (Like, last week, I wanted to reveal but was worried it may backfire in some ways.)

Performing alongside the experienced musicians, always deliver the good stuff and real customer's satisfaction! Or so I thought.

Playing before a British Legion Social Club with a long tradition of strict entertainment etiquettes on stage, the Concert Secretary and his committee members must be shocked to their bones, when the bassist started to gulp down his pint of beer, in between the set.

Earlier at the changing room, I did sound out the importance of being slick on stage with the set-moving smoothly from one song to the next- making us look like professionals!

Guess, I perhaps did not emphasise enough on stage presentation and totally forgot to tell members of the band not to drink on stage.

Not surprisingly, we never got another booking there!

The Music and performance went well and played well by each member of the band but that ' gulping down the pint on stage 'action spoiled it all and it did killed any hope of us ever returning to the club.

A big lesson learned.

Come Together

Organising and putting musicians from a varied and different backgrounds together in a band can have their challenging even tense moments.

At a private summer garden party, the bassist of the group and the female singer had some misunderstandings.

But like true professionals, they kept it under control until the end of the performance, and then, all hell broke loose, in the car park, away from the earshot and view of the many well-heeled and genteel crowd.

Glad to say, months later, on New Year eve, both took the magnanimous step forward to forgive and forget.

They say that in the political world and circle a day is a long time in politics.

Well in the music world, an hour is a long time for musicians. Hence I am able to mix and match different musicians within the hour.

Having practised with them on an individual or group basis, I have compiled their set list with keys of their songs. Therefore, it is a case of calling up to see who is available, putting the appropriate set list, getting the right musicians together for the occasion.

With speedy mobile text, the good old faithful telephone and online email, the response is almost immediate and given the experienced background of each seasoned musician, viola! A band is born, sometimes in an hour.

I once put a band and set together in thirty minutes and played a gig that very night. I use a filing system and have all the set lists of each musician to match.

Having worked with different singers and a wide variety of musicians and having their set list on file, made it possible to form a band in the shortest time possible, over the phone and via email.

Selecting certain similar songs, though in different keys mean it will be easier for all the musicians and singers, as most of them are already in different bands or performing as soloists each week.

To cut down on practice time, each songs in the agreed repertoire has been carefully selected to simplify the whole set list and to get the band as tight as possible.

Following are some of the lead vocalists with the band, The Rhythm Jets, which I formed to take on engagements for pubs, social clubs, parties & weddings.

- » Chantelle Barrow
- » Katie O'Malley,
- » Robert Fisher
- » Beth Anne
- » Amanda Dabrowski
- » Marcus Diamond
- » Jane Fraser
- » Craig Hallsworth
- » Leigh Hitch
- » Phil Tyler
- » Catherine Tyldesley
- » Gina Hunt
- » Garry Flanders
- » Radha
- » John Kelly
- » Steve Francis
- » Danielle

Duos, Trios & Groups I have worked with are:

- » Mick, Dave & Kee
- » The Vanguards with Ian Cooke & Peter Bethell
- » Reload - Nick Curran & Kee
- » Johnny Miller Jazz Trio John Kee & Sarah Prior
- » Marcus & Kee
- » Geoff Nuggent & Kee

- » The Pandas:
- » Amanda Dabrowski
- » Jo Lee
- » Clare McKenzie
- » Rafael Sallon Davies
- » Bien Kee Yeow
- » Steve Francis

Chantelle & The Rhythm Jets.

Barry Collingwood - drums/vocals, Kee –guitar/vocals Chantelle - Vocalist & Ian Edmundson – Bass/vocals.

Set 1:

» I Got Trouble	A
» Drift Away	C#
» Make You Feel My Love	Bb
» Everybody's talking	C
» F B I	A

- » Can't Buy Me Love — C
- » Blueberry Hill — Bb
- » House Of The Rising Sun — Am
- » Apache — Am
- » I'm A Rocker — A
- » A Hard Day's Night — G
- » Help — A
- » Come Together — E

Set 2:

- » FBI — A
- » Back in the USSR — A
- » Stand By Me — A
- » Ain't No Sunshine — Dm
- » Satisfaction — E
- » Proud Mary — D
- » Mustang Sally — C
- » Midnight Hour — E
- » Can't Buy Me Love — C
- » My Girl — C
- » Maggie May — D
- » Hi Ho Silver Lining — D

Encore:

- » Rocking All Over The World — C
- » I Saw Her Standing There — E
- » Gimme Some Lovin — E

Chantelle Barrow

Chantelle Barrow was born into a musical family and has faced many trying challenges in her life since young. Left to fend for herself in her teenage years, because of family issues, she left home whilst still at school. Taking on various jobs to support herself, she used her talent to master various instruments and after graduating with a music degree, she took up solo singing as well as teaching music. Inspiring!

Today she has built a successful career for herself and has her own lovely home and a lovely dog 'max' and is very happy when she is entertaining playing the guitar, violin, keyboard and drums.

Happy to be in two bands with her-The Rhythm Jets & Venus, Jupiter & Mars that perform specially for cafes, bistros and restaurants.

(Repertoire of each Singer: 6 songs highlighted from the Set List)

Fly Me To The Moon, Blueberry Hill, Wonderful World, Billie Jean, Make You Feel My Love, Valerie

Chantelle Barrow –lead vocalist Venus, Jupiter & Mars

Beth Innes & The Rhythm Jets

Beth works with the social service and is the lead vocalist of her own 8pc Soul band 'Big Sister Stuff' based in Manchester.

Her band and her soulful voice is much in demand and weekends will see her and her soulmates busy playing in big social clubs & venues.

Higher & Higher, Get Ready, Money, Uptight, Just My Imagination, Dock of the Bay, Midnight Hour

Ian Edmundson-bass, Brian Roper-drums & Kee-guitar

Wasted Days & Wasted Nights, I Can't Stop Loving You, One Night, FBI.

Geoff & Kee Duo

The late Merseybeat Legend Geoff Nuggent. It was a privilege to have worked with Geoff, a childhood friend of George Harrison.

Geoff Nuggent's band, The Undertaker based in Liverpool, had a record released titled 'Just A Little Bit' and was in the UK Top Singles chart, 1964.

Katie O' Malley & The Rhythm Jets

Get Ready, I'd Rather Go Blind, Knock On Wood, Dancing in the Street, All Along the Watchtower

Katie O Malley

Singer/Songwriter Katie O'Malley is a solo artiste with Spectrum Agency and lead singer with the Rhythm Jets on soul & motown set. She has performed in various festivals, folk clubs & pubs in the North West of England.

Reaching out to her audience, she has carved a name for herself in the local pop and folk scene through her talent and sheer determination.

She has made good and her late Mother would be very proud of her.

Her Father, Superdad Stuart has been a tower of support for her. He assist her in every gig by helping her set up and getting her to and fro from each venue. When you have your Dad as roadie, chauffeur and bodyguard, it is indeed your blessed day!

Graham Hammond and The Rhythm Jets

Graham Hammond, bassist is a full time Teacher in a special needs school in Manchester. Happily married to Lorna, they have a lovely and smart daughter Eva. The future is looking bright for Britain.

Ex-Banker and drummer Brian Roper is the supremo of the drums. His unique drum solo can be heard from Skelsmerdale to Liverpool! There is a video clip of Brian's drum solo of the Ventures 'Wipe Out' on youtube. See Rhythm Jets tag.

Venus, Jupiter & Mars

Clidna – percussions, Chantelle - lead vocalist, Kee-guitar & Craig-drums

Craig Winterburn is a drumming instructor with Treedrum Springstep and he love sharing his skills and knowledge on the various percussions at his centre.

If you are ever in Hulme, Manchester, England and hear the

infectious drum beat in the park, it would most certainly be Craig and his group waking up the neighbourhood.

Hulme used to be a tough neighbourhood with above average unemployment figures in the sixties, but today it has been transformed. The Arts and Music scene has injected a vibrant and more confident mood into the community and Craig is one of the contributors of this change.Craig also debs for the Rhythm Jets as a drummer for the occasional event.

The Blue Pandas

Steve Francis-bass, Amanda, BarryCollingwood-drums, Kee-guitar
Kee –guitar, Clare McKenzie-guitar, Jo, Marcus ,Rafael & Amanda

Amanda Dabrowski & Jo Lee – Hooper
lead vocalists

Beside modelling assignments, Amanda many talents include being a compere for events and she also has a growing business which she runs from her home -'Magic Made Me' taking on artistic assignments like face paintings, statutes, and various marketing projects.

Jo is a multi – talented singer who plays the piano, ukulele, djembe and percussions.

Blue Moon, Besame Mucho, Something Stupid, No Woman No Cry,
Oye Como Va,La Bamba

Jane Frazer & The Rhythm Jets

Blues in A, Stupid Cupid, Proud Mary, Valerie, Summertime, Human
Photo credit: BBC The Voice

Jane Fraser has a regular spot in a Blackpool Seaside Resort, where weekend see her entertaining the many holidaymakers, who flock to Las Vegas of the North.

She is a little Miss Dynamite, with a big voice and has been performing in the North West England pubs & clubs circuit for several years since leaving school. Jane performs with the Rhythm Jets and other bands whenever she gets the opportunity in getting a replacement at her residency. In 2014, she made an appearance on the BBC show 'The Voice.

Marcus Pinnock & Kee Duo

America, Quando, Quando, Quando, Dirty Old Town, Viva Las Vegas, She's a Lady, Dance the Night Away

Marcus Diamond, as his stage name suggest, performs as a Neil Diamond tribute act all over the United Kingdom. Marcus has a tremendous vocalist voice.

He has appeared on X Factor and Britain's Got Talent TV Show and is much in demand in the cabaret /club circuit. Whenever time permit, he performs with various bands to break the 'at times' monotony of going solo. In July 2015 he was chosen for auditions for BBC The Voice.

Lee Hitch & The Rhythm Jets

Leigh Hitch lives in *Leigh!* A Manager with a call centre operation, he is a multi-talented instrumentalist, playing guitar, bass, keyboard and the drums. Leigh deb with various bands and has his own 3piece group, The Good Rebels, playing original materials and the popular covers in pubs, clubs and parties. In July 2015, Lee went over to Sunny Spain to work.

Teenager in Love, Runaway, I Wanna Hold Your Hand, Brown Eyed Girl,

Sex On Fire, Human.

Catherine Tlydesley & The Rhythm Jets

Warwick Avenue, Cry Me A River, Summertime, Perhaps, Perhaps, Perhaps, Top Of The World, Valerie, Back To Black, Close To You

Catherine Tyldesley - Model & Actress.

⟨·CORONATION ST.·⟩

Dedicated and hard working, Catherine focus on her lyrics and melody is to be admired. Her television credits include Holby City, Red Riding, Emmerdale and Florence Nightingale. She played the lead role of Iris Moss in the Liverpool - set BBC One drama, 'Lilies.' Currently she stars in Coronation Street. It has been a privilege to have worked with Catherine, even though she sang as lead vocalist with Rhythm Jets on only two occasions.

Catherine has sung at Manchester United match in Rome and their after games party.

Vocally she is pretty versatile and can handle songs from jazz, swing to pop covers.

Gina Hunt, Garry Flanders & The Rhythm Jets

Gina Hunt is the lead vocalist in the band Rocket 55.

The band play lots of sixties rock n' roll, covers and current top hits. Gina knows a lot about looking good and 'window dressing'. She knows the art very well, as she practice what she preaches - as a window dresser /designer for various top brands /shops.

A Teacher by profession, Garry Flanders teaches music and mathematics in secondary schools & gives private home tuition. Garry plays guitar and keyboards.

Crossroads

Marie's the Name

Roll Over Beethoven

Something

Burning Love

Don't Look Back In Anger

Radha & The Rhythm Jets

Ain't No Sunshine, Leaving On A Jet Plane, Please Mr.Postman, Valerie, Kiss Me

Radha hails from a lovely valley of Wales. University student, Radha is pursuing a full – time course in pharmacy. She is also a part time model. Radha loves music and come the weekend, she can be spotted on certain occasions singing with her friends and also on the club/pub scene, as a solo singer.

She has done some solo spots for spectrum-ktbg agency and has performed in restaurants, bistros, pubs and clubs all over the North West.

Her repertoire cover R&B, Soul & Pop. She is always a big hit with her audience, wherever she goes. Clients tell me, heads are turned, whenever she walks into the room! Radha holds the distinction of being the first artiste in Spectrum Agency to transfer agency commission via internet banking, just after she completed a gig.

Danielle Roper & The Rhythm Jets

A UK School Supply Teacher and Journalist by profession, Danielle Roper took up singing whilst still at school.

Having spend some time in the Republic of Taiwan, she has a

good understanding of China and the Chinese Customs. She hopes to be able to sing some songs and to recite some poems in the mandarin language in the near future.

At the time of completing this book in July 2015, Danielle is putting her journalist skills to good use for a local evening newspapers in Manchester as a Community News Journalist and also as a presenter on Community Radio All FM.

Folsom Prison Blues, Can't Take My Eyes Off You, Money, I'd Rather Go Blind, Superstition

Nick & Kee Duo

All Over Now, Under The Boardwalk, Hero, Spirit In The Sky, Rollercoaster

Who do you call when you need to bury a loved one?

Nick Curran works for a Funeral service company based in Warrington and has seen many tricky situation. Once he was called out to deal with a man who committed suicide and had to pick up body parts on the rail track. To Nick, this was a part of occupational hazard. It was a most tragic sad task. Nick has won a handful of singing awards for his previous duo, Reload.

Johnny Vincent & Kee Duo

Green Green Grass of Home, Gypsy Woman, Sweet Caroline, Little Sister, New York, New York

Johnny Vincent is an established and versatile cabaret Singer who has been in the club entertainment scene for more than forty years.

He has worked with some of the biggest names in the Industry. Billy Fury, Brenda Lee, Duane Eddy, Three Degrees, Peters & Lee, to name just a few. A keen water colour painter, Johnny started his career as a drummer and now plays in a big band in his hometown of Accrington, Lancashire.

Rob Fisher & The Rhythm Jets

Rob Fisher —bass/lead vocalist
Ashley —drums
Kee - guitar
Rob Fisher lead vocalist / bassist is a full time musician based in Sheffield.

He was a member of Chesney Hawkes Band, who had a No.1 hit 'The One and Only' in the UK pop charts in 1991.

Having toured extensively worldwide with the band, Rob now prefers the relatively quieter life as a bass player in a rock band and debbing with various rock and pop bands.

Stone Free, Can't Buy Me Love, Dizzy Miss Lizzy, Heartbreak Hotel, Gimme Some Loving.

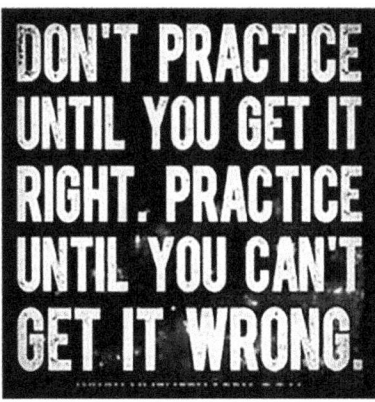

Geoff Nuggent

Merseybeat Legend

Performing with numerous experienced British musicians and meeting patrons has been a rewarding experience and a learning curve for me.

It is an added bonus when I discovered some have played with big names in the music scene. Wow!

Following are just a handful of them.

They are famous ... I very nearly met a Beatle!

Merseybeat Legend and a son of Liverpool, Geoff was a true professional and a gentleman. Come rain, snow or shine, he is always on time for his gigs.

I first met Geoff at the Irlam – Cadishead Summer Festival 2012. My band the Rhythm Jets were on the same billing as his group, The Undertakers fronted by the 60s Vocalist, Jackie Lomax, who had recordings produced by Beatle George Harrison.

Geoff Nuggent and George Harrison were childhood friends growing up in Speke. According to Geoff George used to borrow his guitar on several occasions before he joined the Beatles.

His first group, the Vegas Five was one of the first Rock n' Roll bands in Liverpool. The Undertakers single record release 'Just A Little Bit' was in the Top 50 UK Single Charts 1964 – youtube.

Friends and top Liverpool musicians paid tribute to him at his funeral service October 2014 by singing his favourite songs. They described him as a brilliant musician and praised his work in raising thousands for local charities over the years.

It has been a privilege to have got to know Geoff and have performed on stage with him –an absolute diamond. During our break time after the first set, I will listened intently to his wonderful tales of his days with George Harrison, the exciting times in ex-Beatle Pete Best's Casbah Club and his band in Star Club Hamburg 1962- the same venue where the Beatles played

Guess this is the closest one would get to the company of the Beatles –a dream come true!

Jail'ouse Rock

Johnny R (stage name)

Cabaret Singer & Still Life Artist

Johnny R has been in the music circle since the modern baby pampers were introduced in England.

Battling through a very troubled childhood, plagued with family problems and failed relationships peppered with a criminal record, life looks bleak for Johnny R.

He was doing badly in school, often playing truants and hated going there. All Teachers were a nuisance to Johnny R.

'What do they do, them Wankers except to give us grief 'he used to think whilst growing up.

His troubled upbringing has moulded him into this angry rebel and he hated authority.

In class he was the chief trouble maker, often encouraging the others to disrupt the lessons by swearing,throwing things about and relished the looks of frustration on his Teacher's face when there is a breakdown in class order.

His shoplifting adventures soon progressed to more serious acts of criminal activities.He was soon in a gang that broke into property and on many occasions stole cars for joy riding.

Joy riding is a teenage act of taking a car for a high speed drive, and suddenly pulling up the handbrakes, to spin the car around and breaking out in ecstasy and laughter!

Soon he found himself in prison after assaulting a pensioner for his pension money.

While serving his sentence, he started singing in his cell to pass the time away.

Many inmates commented and praised his singing and said he had a good voice.

Inmate : 'Eh....mate you got a sick voice' (sick in northern english slang means good)

Johnny R: 'Tar mate, its summat to do,init?

Inmate: 'You should should f...... join X factor and get f...... known '

Johnny R: 'Don't be a F...... wanker, how can I?

Inmate: 'Why not matey? '

Johnny R: 'Becos, I am F.......bang up in here, ain't I! ? Stop talking Shite,you C...'

(*Writer's note: I have typed dash...... as I cannot bring myself to spelling or saying the F or C word.In my entire life I have only said the F word perhaps a dozen times*)

But sing he did, daily, without fail in his cell behind bars, until he was released after a year.

A chance meeting with a school mate after he came out from 'the nick' according to Johnny changed his life. This friend, a musician encouraged Johnny to join in the weekly open-mic session at the local pub. Local musicians meet to chat and anyone who wishes to sing or play an instrument can go on stage to do so.

Johnny urged on by his friend Colin took his first big step and sang three numbers to the delight of all that night. The Landlord who was suitably impressed with his vocal range and singing offered him a weekly paid spot.

All he needed to be ready to do paid gigs were a set of 2 x 45 mins.set of songs, PA system,

backing tracks for self- contained artiste and transport.

'I could not believe my bleeding luck' he told me.

'Where the hell was I going to get some backing tracks' he wondered at that point of time.

Luckily for Johnny there was an in –house PA system he could use as he was broke. And again, step forward his good friend Colin, who loaned him some backing tracks. Johnny V was on the way!

He took up the opportunity that was there and never looked back and continued till this day.

Staying away from his old criminal pals after coming out of the 'nick ' and going into singing in clubs and pubs was the best decision he made he confessed to me.

It appears that those long and lonely hours spent behind bars singing had finally paid off for Johnny R and his decision to stay with the positive side of things changed his life for the better.

I first met Johnny R at a centre where I was teaching students who have been expelled from school for bad behaviour. They attended daily for games and lessons.

Johnny V joined my artistes agency a few months after our meeting and has continued to performed as a solo artiste ever since. The feedback from his performances have all been positive.

The future now looks bright and orange for Johnny R!

I can see clearly now, the rain is gone,

I can see all obstacles in my way,

Gone are the dark clouds that had me blind,

It's gonna be a bright, bright sunshiny day.

Jimmy Cliff Singer/Songwriter

Be of good cheer. Do not think of today's failures, but of the success that may come tomorrow. You have set yourselves a difficult task, but you will succeed if you persevere; and you will find a joy in overcoming obstacles. Remember, no effort that we make to attain something beautiful is ever lost.

Helen Keller Author, Lecturer, Activist

Chick, Drummer

What a cheeky name! Chick is walking testimony that age is no barrier when it comes to music and performing live on stage.

There is still a lot of musical life yet in this Veteran of the battle of the bands! Having lived through two world wars, Chick is not about to give up his passion for drumming.

'They don't bother me. The current boom, boom, boom monotonous bass and drum beat with boring repetitions. In them days, it was bomb, bomb, bomb and more bombs from them Germans: now that was scary!'

It was at a band gig that I met Chick and his family from Bolton. The town that gave the world Samuel Crompton and his invention 'the spinning mule' a machine that revolutionised the spinning industry. A true blue Lancashire Lad, Chick and his lovely wife Joanne, an established Singer has just returned after a few years performing in Spain in a jazz/swing group.

This meeting led me to calling on Chick to deb on a few occasions and he has been the driving force behind the beat of Venus, Jupiter and Mars –a three piece trio playing mainly covers.

Veteran drummer Chick has played in many venues since leaving school. He has backed big names in UK Showbiz music industry. Big names like Tom Jones, Englebert Humperdinck ('they were unknown and worked under a different name then')Peters & Lee, Billy Fury ,Marty Wilde ,Des O' Connor, Matt Munro and the list of who is who goes on.... The Mecca of the North England in those days of the sixties was Talk of The North and many weekends saw Chick playing there either as a resident drummer or with his group.

At his age Chick is an inspiration to all Musicians –old and young alike! His drumming is just so brilliant and perfection. He has developed his own style and watching him play is a joy!

You don't have to put away your equipment, talent and retire during the weekend watching Strictly Come Dancing and munching pop corns at home, when you can be on stage doing the thing you love most – performing and watching young and matured ladies watching and admiring you!

It must be a great feeling and we joked about it during our breaks.

Last word from Good Old Chick 'Like my hearing aid, it's like, getting your battery re-charged!'

North England in those days of the sixties was Talk of The North and many weekends saw Chick playing there either as a resident drummer or with his group.

At his age Chick is an inspiration to all Musicians –old and young alike! His drumming is just so brilliant and perfection. He has developed his own style and watching him play is a joy!

You don't have to put away your equipment, talent and retire during the weekend watching Strictly Come Dancing and munching pop corns at home, when you can be on stage doing the thing you love most – performing and watching young and matured ladies watching and admiring you!

It must be a great feeling and we joked about it during our breaks.

Last word from Good Old Chick 'Like my hearing aid, it's like, getting your battery re-charged!'

Ian Edmundson – Bassist Supremo

Brian Roper-drums, Katie O Malley –lead vocalist, Ian Edmundson – bass, Kee-guitar

Nothing comes better baked than Ian Edmundson. He truly knows his stuff and is a seasoned musician. I came into contact with Ian through another guitarist Steve Mulvaney with the pink Floyd tribute band.

Steve and Ian were in the Kerbcrawlers, a top local band who did the odd gigs with my agency spectrum-ktbg.

After the band broke up, I approach Ian if he could help out on bass with the Rhythm Jets a kind of scratch band.

I learned this 'scratch' term from him. The term means putting various musicians to play for the occasional functions.

Whenever I provided the name of the venue we were due to play to him, Mr. Done It All and Seen It All Ian will go:

'I have played there years ago' and 'been there, done that'

Almost every pubs and clubs seemed to have had his serene presence there previously, and he has plugged his amp in the same electrical sockets!

So I guessed this guy knows what he is talking about.

My father used to tell me.' Always work with someone who is better than you, if you want to learn and improve yourself.'

How true those words were.

Besides sharing his knowledge about chord structures Ian made a good impression on me on how a neat stage is essential. The audience will have a better impression of the whole band if we all look good in our best presentation and, the stage is not cluttered with guitar cases, drum cases, bags, plastic bags handbags, of the female singer, umbrellas, water bottles and half eaten sandwiches.

Once we had a singer who had wires running all over the stage, like he was setting up a 'trip and die' trap for us.

I could not help laughing when I saw the agony on Ian Edmundson's face! He grinned and remarked 'It looks like a f...... Steptoe and Son junkyard here on stage!'

I did not know who this Steptoe TV Character was. The magical world of Google told me during the break, and I had a bigger laugh!

Back home we have all the PA system, amplifiers, speakers drum set supplied and set up by a company. We walk on stage like big stars carrying only our guitars and drum sticks. Hence it was useful to learn how to set up the band stage. Thanks to him, I am more conscious now how a good set up and band stage presentation should be.

After a while performing with Ian, I found out he guest performed with two of UK most famous bands – Slade and Bay City Rollers.

You know Christmas is coming when you hear 'And here it is, Merry Christmas everybody is having fun ...' by Slade.

I don't really follow their music so had very little knowledge of their music. Still, I can boast to my folks back home that I have performed with someone who has played with these two UK household named bands.

Peter, the Parking Lord

'Oh Lord, it's hard to be humble, and parked perfect in everyway...'

'Excuse me, can I park here for an extra hour?' I asked the parking attendant, a kind looking gentleman at a village supermarket, after doing my shopping.

This was the beginning of an acquaintance with Peter. After several parking's at the convenient spot for over a year, I stopped one day to chat to Peter as it was starting to snow.

'Goodness Peter, have you seen how fast the snow is falling?' I asked him as he was putting on a raincoat.

'Yes, it is jolly furious!' he replied.

After our initial exchange of pleasantries I asked him about his job and past working experience ,like I usually do being extra interested in people 'who do me favours' (like allowing me free parking)

To my utter astonishment Peter revealed a little secret He was a past member of the Royal Household.

He recounted after some prodding how he got the kitchen job at Buckingham Palace, after an interview in London and how he rose to be a purser to HRH Prince Andrew.

Peter laughed when he mentioned the occasion when Prince Andrew picked him out of a crowd, on a Royal Navy Ship duty, after he has left the job at the Royal Household.

'I was in a line with my mates to welcome the Prince on board to inspect the new navy ship and he looked at me, pointed me out to my immediate Officer and said, 'I know this chap, he used to work for me' At that very moment, Peter said with a smile on his face that they both broke out laughing!

To further surprise me, Peter went on to proudly show me something he pulled out from his pocket. I really was floored when I saw it. It was a form of I.D. stating he was made a Lord of the Realm. Yes, Peter was a Lord of Her Majesty, the Queen's Realm. He was bestowed the lordship for services to the Royal Household.

Oh Lord, it is really a humbling experience to know that the quiet parking attendant, Peter once walked the corridors of power in Buckingham Palace.

This is the closest I got to shake the hands of British Royalty via Lord Peter.

Dining at Windsor Castle.

Some interesting facts to take note, if you ever get an invitation to dine with Her Majesty, Queen.

- » Windsor Castle guests dine at a massive table which seats 160 people. Table made in 1846.
- » Takes 2 days to lay the table—2,000 pieces of silver gilt cutlery and 960 glasses.
- » Each guest has six glasses.
- » One Man folds all the 170 napkins.
- » Windsor Castle has the oldest working kitchen in Britain.
- » The Walls and ceilings of St.George's hall are covered with colourful heraldic crests of each member of the Order of the Garter. The blanks ones are those of disgraced knights.
- » Nobody start their meals until the Hosts –the Queen and Duke of Edinburgh start to eat.

You never know who you will meet at a gig - When Jo Met Marion

The day Veteran Soldier Jo met Marion Mitchell Morrison will forever be etched in his mind and memory. Marion Morrison was no ordinary Jo Blogg. Marion's other name was John Wayne, or the Duke, the global iconic Cowboy movie star.

This chance meeting took place in a bar in Tripoli, Libya 1957 on one of Jo's day off while serving in the army there. Striking up a conversation with the Duke after he greeted them warmly even though they were total strangers, Jo was over the moon to meet his idol. He has seen every one of John Wayne's movies. Now coming face to face with his idol was surreal. He could not believe his British Bull Dog Luck!

Finding out that Jo and his fighting comrades were fighting the bad guys, (just like his role in his cowboy movies) John Wayne invited them to next day's filming of 'Legend of the Lost' in the desert. Upon arrival they landed a double bonus. Marion introduced them to his co-star Sophia Loren.

To Jo and his soldier comrades, that day in the hot desert of Libya, in the ruins of the Leptis Magna, God smiled on them. To have met two huge stars of the screen and to watch their movie in action was like striking gold! Relating this incredible story, I could see the twinkle in Jo's eyes –all so tearful and joyous at the same time. All I asked Jo earlier as I usually do, when my band performs in a new town was 'Is there anybody or anything famous from this town?'

To which he replied 'Yes, Russell Watson and me.'

What a story Jo, and I am pleased that I could tell my folks back home, I have met and shook the hand of the man, who shook the hand of Marion Mitchell Morrison!

A mix of Inspirational music lyrics matching with the occasion and moment

Music quotes and sayings by music lovers and musicians that will provide insights, lessons and reflections into life, both in relationship with others and also with ourselves as individuals.

Sad songs, happy songs, love songs, songs to empower, anti-war songs, and songs for all occasions are ways musicians communicate their messages.

These messages are inspired from spirit /soul to assist us on life's journey.

Music reaches out and can touch, heal, inspire and soothes the soul.

Love and Relationship

- Total Eclipse of the Moon: Enigma
- I just called to say I love you: Stevie Wonder
- Have I told you lately that I love you: Rod Stewart
- Truly: Lionel Ritchie
- Make you feel my love: Adele
- And I Love her: The Beatles
- Ain't No Sunshine: Bill Withers
- Can't Help Falling: Elvis Presley
- Wonderful Tonight: Eric Clapton
- Heartbreak Hotel: Elvis Presley
- The Great Pretender: The Platters
- Quando, Quando, Quando : Michael Buble
- Words: The Bee Gees
- To Love Somebody: The Bee Gees
- Love on the Rock : Neil Diamond
- Walk Right Back: The Everly Brothers
- Knock Three Times: Dawn
- No Woman, No Cry: Bob Marley
- Will You Still Love Me Tomorrow: The Shirelles
- Something: George Harrison
- I Left My Heart in San Francisco: Tony Bennett
- I Can't Stop Loving You: Ray Charles
- Something Stupid: Frank & Nancy Sinatra
- I Will Always love You: Whitney Houston
- Unchained Melody: The Righteous Brothers

- » Mona Lisa: Nat King Cole
- » Love Is A Many Splendour Thing : Nat King Cole
- » Solemente Una Vez : Andrea Bocelli
- » Besame Mucho: Consuelo Velasquez
- » Blue Moon: Billy Eckstine & Mel Torme
- » Let It Be Me: The Everly Brothers
- » Maggie May: Rod Stewart
- » Help: The Beatles
- » Something Good: Herman Hermits
- » Blueberry Hill: Fats Domino
- » My Girl: The Temptations
- » Are You Lonesome Tonight: Elvis Presley
- » Love Me Tender: Elvis Presley
- » Here There And Everywhere: Paul McCartney

Environment / Humanitarian/Spiritual Awareness Song Lyrics

- » Give Peace A Chance: John Lennon & Yoko Ono
- » Imagine: John Lennon
- » The Logical Song: Supertramp

Encouragement, Life & Hope Song Lyrics

- » Everybody Hurts: R.E.M
- » Hand in my Pocket: Alanis Morissette
- » Somewhere Over The Rainbow: Various Artistes
- » What a Wonderful World: Louis Armstrong
- » Three Little Birds: Bob Marley
- » Que Sera Sera: Doris Day
- » New York, New York: Frank Sinatra
- » I Can See Clearly Now: Jimmy Cliff
- » The Young Ones: Cliff Richard
- » Green Green Grass of Home: Tom Jones
- » Ce Le Vie: Chuck Berry
- » All My Loving : The Beatles

Dark Songs / Sad Songs / Anticipation

- » Bad Moon Rising: Creedence Clearwater Revival
- » Leaving On A Jet Plane: The Carpenters

Happy / Celebrations / Friendship

- » Celebration: Kool & The Gang
- » That's Amore: Dean Martin
- » Sway: Michael Buble
- » Happy Happy Birthday Baby: Tuneweavers

Beach / Pool Songs

- » Surfin' USA: Beach Boys
- » I Get Around: Beach Boys
- » Under The Boardwalk: The Drifters

Friendship

- » You've Got A Friend: James Taylor
- » With A Little Help From My Friends: Ringo Starr
- » Wind Beneath My Wings: Bette Midler

Family

- » We Are Family: Sister Sledge
- » Dance With My Father: Luther

Please Don't Let Me Be Misunderstood

Mixed & Matched up Wrongly
When 2 Singaporeans & 1 Malaysian collide with I Englishman

When two cultures collide, misunderstandings can turn out to be catastrophic than that time your mother put Chinese soya sauce in your fish and chips!

Most Northern English like their fish and chips spiced with salt, vinegar and tomato ketchup.

An episode on a British TV Documentary, UK Border Force shone a light on this clash of cultures and the unfortunate misunderstanding that ensures.

The show takes viewers behind the scenes of the Immigration process and shot at Heathrow Airport. It reveal the methods and technology employed to catch illegal entry to the UK.

Watching this particular episode involving three newly arrived passengers-one Malaysian and two from Singapore, who face the prospect of being denied entry, I am convinced it was all a cultural misunderstanding —on the part of the Immigration Officer.

The dialogue between one of the Singaporean Visitor (SV) and the Immigration Officer (IO) went along something like this, after they were stopped and taken aside.

- » IO: Why are you all here?
- » SV: Holiday Ma.
- » IO: Why, you have relatives here?
- » SV: No, Just come to see see England. Everybody say very nice.
- » IO: So what are you all planning to see?
- » SV : There, got the thing lo, the, the Queen house ah ,where she is staying and also go looking around and see ,what good to see ma, museum, Chinatown and many many places. I also not too sure, my friend in London will show us.
- » IO: The Gentleman you are travelling with, Is he your relative?
- » SV: No, No, Just a friend only.
- » IO: How long have you known him?
- » SV: Only few weeks ago. Met him on holiday.
- » IO: We noticed you have been checking his passport and telling him what to say, when you were all queuing up, earlier.
- » SV: Ya, he cannot speak English Ma! So I help him.
- » IO: Why were you holding his passport?
- » SV: I say already, I help him, because he cannot understand

English.

» IO: You have brought so many shirts and even ties for a five day holiday. If I go on holiday, I don't bring along a tie and for 5 day stay, I would not bring 12 shirts. Are you here for a job interview?

» SV: No, No, I Sweat ma, I sweat a lot, so I need changing. For the tie, not for interview but I want to wear tie to look smart. Because I see on TV, the Europeans look very smart, when they go out, wearing tie.

The above is just a transcript from my memory of the exchange between the Immigration Officer and the Singaporean Visitor transmitted on TV.

After consulting his senior, the Immigration Officer informed the visitors that they will all be denied entry based on grounds they are not genuine holidaymakers.

What an unfortunate outcome.

The two Singaporeans and a Malaysian are all above 60 years old, and this, from my personal point of view is purely a collision of the cultural kind. It is not uncommon for us to go on holiday with people we have just met.

Majority of folks living under the tropical sun would just prefer to jet off somewhere cool .They would not be planning or strategizing each and every minute or hour of their pending trip. The elder folks just want to get out and see a different scenery and not too bothered about the finer details.

Singapore is a flat but very prosperous island nation. There are no high rise mountains, no natural waterfalls, very humid and stifling hot, being right on the equator and it would be a nice change to experience a different landscape.

It is quite natural in eastern culture to greet people from back home and show them round a new city or invite them along for a holiday. The English, being rather reserved, find the idea of taking someone you just met for a holiday rather strange! Some can't even stand their own partners at times, never mind others. As for checking the passports of friends, again, this can be quite an innocent act. We tend to help our country folks, if they don't understand the language and will advise them how to answer any immigration questions or help them fill in the required entry form. A no, no action while waiting to be screened by immigration control, unless you are super famous!

All these actions and gestures caught on airport CCTV security cameras can arouse suspicions and raised the alarm bells! It was a wrong decision to exclude them from entering the UK, based on the answers and the behaviour of the Singaporeans. The Immigration Clearance Officer should have been more sensitive to the difference in cultures and taken into account the age and the language difficulty of the banned but actually 'genuine' visitors.

This is a classic case of mixed up and matched up wrongly perceptions of two cultures.

Mix & Matching Up Christian Names for Chinese

You can call me AL

My English friends have asked me "Hi Kee, why do so many of your Chinese people like taking on an English Christian name?"

I really do not know why for sure, but based on childhood experiences, I have a hunch that the reasons why Chinese people in Singapore, Malaysia and Hong Kong in particular like adopting English names is because for the following varied reasons below:

» Historic link with Colonial Masters, Great Britain. Everything made or associated with England is seen to be superior. Be it shoes, clothes, music, brands, products and especially education.

» Taking on an English name like Alfred Ho, Winston Tan, Andrew Wan, Charles Wong, Diana Chan, Elizabeth Kee, Matthew Lim, Mary Chong can all sound very nice, regal and even religious.

» Sounding nice. See the instant difference when a Chinese real name is given cosmetic treatment.

Fatt You Ho - Alfred Ho
Cheet To Tan -Winston Tan
Too Long Wan – Andrew Wan
Fok Yew Wong - Charles Wong
Go Loo Chan - Diana Chan
Tong Chong Kee- Elizabeth Kee
Been Sin Lim – Matthew Lim
Sek Si Chong – Mary Chong

» For Convenience. Many Chinese people especially those in business and sales use their adopted English names as a communication tool. It is easy to remember and very convenient, and most important to these 'money minded' tight as two paint of coats people It is free!

» International Flavour –An English name can have some advantages in English speaking country.

When I was a kid, most of my Chinese friends have taken on Christian names, even when they are not Christians by religion. So my brothers suggested a few from the bible for me. I nearly ended with the name Moses. The idea that he had power to divide the seas was just tempting. Now that would be an impressive name! In the end I settled for a less powerful but rocky name, Peter.

Jackie Chan birth and real name is Fong Si Lung. For personal reasons he had to change his surname to Chan. He got the nickname Jackie from a working colleague, whilst working on a construction site to supplement his income as a stuntman in early kung fu movies.

Top 10 Boys and Girls names for 2014 in England

- 1 Jack
- 2 Oliver
- 3 Charlie
- 4 Harry
- 5 Jacob
- 6 Alfie
- 7 Noah
- 8 Oscar
- 9 George
- 10 James
- 1 Amelia
- 2 Olivia
- 3 Emily
- 4 Isla
- 5 Ava
- 6 Poppy
- 7 Sophie
- 8 Jessica
- 9 Lily
- 10 Sophia

Keep on Running
Some Tips to avoid tripping over for Musicians

'Oh no, I have left my car keys in the car!'

'Oh dear, I forgot the leads for the PA speakers and the stands as well.'

We have had similar experience which left us in a dire straits and hopefully a few suggestions here could be helpful-for the busy and not the not so very organised musicians, who only focus on playing music and sounding good on stage.

Car Keys

Leave a spare car key in your guitar case or equipment bag, in case you are locked out or in the event you left your car key inside the boot or car when you were unloading at the gig venue.

If at a practice in a studio / someone's house, keep your car keys with your shopping or personal effects. I have kept my car key with the butter, a bottle of milk and a packet of pork chops I bought for dinner, in the bass guitarist's home fridge, while we were practicing at his home, so as not to forget to take home after the practice.

Tired Eyes

For very busy musician (eat, listen and rest all at the same time)

Try closing your eyes well and listen to the music you will be playing in a couple of hours, to refresh those difficult lyrics and have a better feel of the songs. and eating at the same time, so as to relax and put your feet up as you do.

Emergency List of Musicians

Have a written list of musicians with you, on your mobile or in a book, just in case you need them in an emergency situation-the drummer or singer can't make it at the last minute.

I always have stand-by Musicians, DJs for big & important event especially New Year Eve or Wedding.

Weddings and New Year Eve are two very important events and it is wise to have contingency plan (plan B) should the unexpected happen. It is a big day!

Health & Safety

Taped down securely all wires at gigs.

This is to avoid anyone falling over or tripping any wires especially if there are children or vulnerable people around.

Speakers and stands should have a secured wide base at all times and placed in a secured area. Make sure no one is sitting near heavy speakers for Health & Safety measure, especially young children or pets.

Don't miss out on your pay

Don't discuss any problems relating to the set list or any other band issues in the presence of staff or the Manager /Landlord of the venue.

Turning up to set up for a gig, the drummer started to introduce himself to the others whom he has just met.' 'Goodness, you are better looking than the person I spoke to on the phone.' Eddie said to Rob the bassist. 'It's a good job, we had the discussion and went over the songs over the phone, or we will not have a clue what to play and may screw up big time tonight!

The set went well as all the musicians were experienced session musicians and the crowd generally happy with the band.

After packing up and expecting their pay, the Landlord approached the band and instead of handing us the cash, he started to remind us that we were a band put together at the last minute and wanted a discount. He also pointed out his takings were not that good that evening and was trying to find some excuse not to pay the full fee as agreed. After much haggling, (and bassist making some strange boast) a discounted sum was handed over, reluctantly by him. Not all Landlords behave in this manner but why give them some excuse not to pay

Handshakes should be warm

Going to an appointment with a prospect for the very first time, it is always a good idea to warm your hands in your trousers pocket or even a radiator, on a very cold winter day, before you shake hands.

It will convey a warm feeling and personality and may just tip the end result in your favour.

Speeding, Loading equipment and parking

Check to make sure it is safe and legal where you stop to unload the equipment and then the place where you park your vehicle.

On the way to the gig drive with care and watch your speed. To forfeit your hard earned cash for a speeding, loading or parking fine can be hard to accept.

Always call ahead to make sure they clear the space for loading and to clear the tables and chairs, where the band/artiste performs.

Problematic patrons

Majority are out to have a pleasant entertaining evening but the odd individual or a small group may be a bit challenging especially when they are a bit tipsy and wanting to grab the microphone thinking they are on Britain's Got Talent. The best solution is to alert the Landlord/Manager of the venue and usually some action will resolve it.

The contracted time & details

Keep to what has been agreed with regard to the type of songs expected and the makeup of the band and the agreed time of performance.

Artiste & Bands have a better chance of being asked to return if they are crowd pleasers. Patrons should not beg for that extra song, even after the encore. It is all about them not the musicians, really.

Spare instruments & other spares & essentials.

Keep them near and handy.

Extra guitar strings, spare guitar, extra guitar leads, amplifier fuses, additional microphone, plasters for cut or sore fingers and some other medical needs, snacks, water, maps, notepads, pens, car breakdown cover and a fully charged mobile phone especially travelling to functions miles away from home

And not forgetting a bottle of water, especially for people like me, who make at least 100 calls a day prospecting for work for the band and the artistes-the ideal staff for a call centre.

Should the worst thing happen, like your amplifier fails-put your guitar through the PA system.

Giving Satisfaction

Customers normally would want more music, particularly if the band or singer goes down really well.

Not to play the extra numbers would surely disappoint them. Quite often even if the band has played two or three extra songs as the encore, there are still some patrons who will shout out for one more or two more.

To keep customers satisfied and go home with broad smiles, it may be a good idea to announce earlier, in the last set, just before you do the encore numbers (2 songs before the encore numbers) that these two numbers are the last songs. So when it finishes, and the call for more can be satisfied by the encore numbers

Otherwise an encore can drag on and on. All good things must come to an end

As I am typing this, a report on the Radio sadly confirmed that over 4,000 pubs will close in the next year 2014.

According to the Good Pub Guide 2014, it is actually good news for the Industry. The closing of 'bad pubs' that offer unimaginative food and drink will give visionary and energetic licensees a chance to open new ones. It will give a much needed shot in the arm and make the pub industry more robust and better placed for the future.

It is forecast that between 2,500 and 4,000 pubs are to close in 2014 and more than a 1,000 new ones will open.

There is hope in a Crisis. The Mandarin word for crisis composed of two words - Danger and Opportunity.

The Chinese believe that there are opportunities in the wording- as one can turn danger and threat to a good force and opportunity.

Crisis in Mandarin

Wei –Chi
Wei - danger & Chi- opportunity

Speaking Words of Wisdom

Chinese Philosopher Confucius, 551-479BC, was a very wise Chinese thinker and social philosopher, whose teachings and philosophy have deeply influenced Chinese thoughts on the education and compartment of the ideal man; how such an individual should live his life and interact with others, and the form of society and the government in which he should participate.

Confucius' influence in Chinese history has been compared to that of Socrates in the west.

Quotes of Confucius, born 551B.C. - 479B.C.

- » Everything has its beauty but not everyone sees it.
- » It does not matter how slowly you go, so long as you do not stop.
- » A journey of a thousand miles begin with the first step.
- » Our greatest glory is not in never falling, but in getting up every time we do.
- » What you do not want done to yourself, do not do to others.
- » Choose a job you love, and you will never have to work a day in your life.

Quotes of other Wisemen of the Far East

- » It does not matter if the cat is black or white, so long as it catch the mice. Deng Hsiao Ping, Communist Party Leader
- » A person without a smiling face should not open a shop. Lee Kay Loon
- » An old broom has its value. Ching Lai Huat
- » The old horse will know the way. Cheong Kah Thong
- » Do not wait until you are thirsty, to dig a well. Si Fu Tzu

» It is better to walk alone, than follow a crowd going in the wrong direction. Low Si Fu

Below are some ancient Confucius sayings and their modern interpretations.

» **Your future depend on your dreams.**

   Don't waste any time, go to bed now! (After a tiring gig, take a nice warm bath, nice hot cocoa and go to bed – musicians like chilling out till early morning and don't get enough sleep)

» **Man who want pretty nurse, must be patient.**

   All good things come to those who wait.

» **Man who leaps off cliff jumps to conclusion.**

   You must assess your situation before deciding or result can be disastrous.

» **War does not determine who is right, it determines who is left.**

   Might seem to be right, however unjust.

» **Man who drive like hell is bound to get there.**

   Ignorance and determination sometimes gets you the result.

» **Man who live in glass house should change clothes in basement.**

   Do not wash your dirty linens in public.

» **When the big tree fall, all monkeys run away!**

   When elephants fight, the little insignificant mouse gets trampled.

» **Men wouldn't lie as much to the women in their life, if the women in their life didn't ask so many questions!**

   Be sure your sins will find you out!

Not on my Wedding Day

Performing at a wedding function is the most wonderful experience for some musicians and nerve wrecking for others. The selection of the appropriate songs are very important and some thoughts should be given to the choice of songs. Getting suggestions from the happy couple will certainly help. It is such a special occasion where the ambience and elegantly dressed guests, the newlyweds and their friends and families all combined to make it a day to remember forever.

Here's some tips for the first timers to the wedding event. An understanding of how it works, the right selection of songs help set the mood and style for the proceedings.

Before the Ceremony:

Starting off on a light note, usually some jazz numbers and sweet songs. The music played should be light and cheerful-jazz or classical and cross over styles

Procession:

The Musician should have a good view from where one is seated and tell the minister to give you a nod when it's time to start each section. Request to be seated where you can see the beginning of the aisle. You have to watch for who's walking and play the appropriate music piece-Groomsmen & Bridesmaids, Flower Girls/Ring Girl.

Bride:

The Bride always get her own choice of music, while walking down the aisle accompanied by her Father or other family members.

Minister/vows:

Musicians will need to stop playing within 30 secs of the bride reaching the front. No music while the Minister is speaking.

Signing:

Being the quietest part of the ceremony, where the bridegroom, minister and witnesses go to sign the wedding document.

Music is usually played at this point of the event.

Pronouncement:

A couple of final words from the minister, then to the lovey dovey part-the kiss!

Walk away:

The grand 'Ave Maria' bride and groom walking down the aisle as Man and Wife to the claps and cheers. To add to the excitement and the wonderful occasion, play something cheerful and upbeat.

Always check and adjust accordingly at wedding functions. When in doubt, it will be a good idea to attend the dress rehearsal.

Some tips for playing at a wedding function:

Be well rehearsed and prepared like the motto of the Scouts.

Pre-arranged payment for your service-who to pay you at the wedding.

Music selection: Inform the Bride and Groom what music to expect and get them to select their favourites.

Buy a wedding music book-it has arrangement for the various parts of the wedding. Check out 'Wedding music for any instrument.' via Amazon.

Hand-out your business cards on the day to the wedding planner, venue manager, catering company for future work.

Relax and enjoy playing. Everyone is there for the wedding and the focus is on the bride and groom.

Suggestions for the music selection:

The Processional (Bridal entrance)

- » The Arrival of the Queen Of Sheba
- » Trumpet Voluntary in D (H.Purcell)

- » Trumpet Tune (H.Purcell)
- » March (G F. Handel)
- » Butterfly Waltz Brian Crain
- » Bridal Chorus (Here Comes The Bride)
- » Grand March From Aida Verdi

For Bride:

- » Canon in D (J.Pachelbel)
- » The Bridal Chorus (R Wagner)
- » Wedding March (A midsummer night)

Signing

- » Ave Maria (Bach /Gounod)
- » Instrumentals

Walk away

- » The Wedding March by Mendelssohn
- » Ode to Joy L.Beethoven

Reception & Wedding Dinner Repertoire

Medley of Beautiful Instrumental Piano Music Puccini's Nessun Dorma, Tchaikovsky's The Sleeping Beauty, Table For Four, Canoe, Responsible For You, Falling Star, Red Sails In The Sunset and Blue Moon.

» Take Five	Dave Brubeck Quartet
» Fly Me To The Moon	Frank Sinatra
» Besame Mucho	Andrea Bocelli
» Love Me Tender	Elvis Presley
» Girl from Ipanema	A.Gilberto & Stan Getz

- » I'm In The Mood For Love — Ella Fitzgerald
- » Blue Moon — Julie London
- » Let It Be Me — Everly Brothers
- » All My Loving — The Beatles
- » Summertime — Norah Jones
- » The Shadow of Your Smile — George Benson
- » Mona Lisa — Nat King Cole
- » Solemente Una Vez — Andrea Bocelli
- » Quando Quando Quando — Michael Buble
- » Misty — Johnny Mathis
- » I Get A Kick Out Of You — Frank Sinatra
- » Here There And Everywhere — The Beatles
- » Love Is A Many Splendour Thing — Nat King Cole
- » Pachelbel's — Canon in D
- » Theme For Young Lover — The Shadows
- » One Step — Michael DelGuidice
- » Have I Told You Lately — Rod Stewart

Choosing the first dance song and evening repertoire is a very personal choice but having played at over a hundred wedding parties, these are some of the popular choice of the wedding couple.

Top 'First Dance' & Wedding Songs

- » God Must Have Spent A Little Time More On You - NSYNC
- » The Wedding Song — Ave Maria Julie Rogers
- » Love — Nat King Cole
- » The Way You Look Tonight — Michael Buble

- » Amazed — Lone Star
- » At Last — Celine Dion
- » Now That I Found You — Dawna Johnson
- » Unchained Melody — The Righteous Brothers
- » From This Moment — Shania Twain
- » Angels — Robbie Williams
- » Have I Told You Lately — Rod Stewart
- » I Will Always Love You — Whitney Houston
- » I Don't Wanna Miss a Thing — Aerosmith
- » The Power Of Love — Celine Dion
- » Endless Love — Lionel Richie
- » Let It Be Me — Everly Brothers
- » At Last — Etta James
- » Unforgettable — Nat King Cole
- » Love Me Tender — Elvis Presley
- » Because You Loved Me — Celine Dion
- » That's Amore — Dean Martin
- » Thank God I Found You — Mariah Carey
- » Heaven In Your Eyes — Lover Boy
- » Can't Help Falling in Love — Elvis Presley
- » Moon River — Andy Williams
- » Crazy — Patsy Cline
- » Sway — Dean Martin
- » Frozen in Time — James Collins
- » I Will Always Love You — Whitney Houston

- » Angels — Robbie Williams
- » Truly Madly Deeply — Savage Garden
- » From This Moment — Shania Twain
- » You're Still The One I Love — Shania Twain
- » To Make You Feel My Love — Adele
- » You're Beautiful — James Blunt
- » A Thousand Years — Christine Perry
- » Never Be Alone — Nickleback
- » Mirrors — Justin Timblelake
- » Fallin' — Alicia Keys
- » Marry Me — Train
- » I Do It For You — Bryan Adams
- » Norah Jones — Come Away With Me
- » The Lady In Red — Chris deBurgh
- » Can You Feel The Love Tonight — Elton John
- » Marry You — Bruno Mars
- » Everything — Michael Buble

Walking down the aisle songs

- » The Wedding Song — Ave Maria
- » Endless Love — Mariah Carey
- » I Won't Give Up — Jason Mraz
- » I Swear — Nick Lachey
- » Unchained Melody — Righteous Brothers

Some songs not to play at a wedding

- But I still haven't found what I was looking for — U2
- Don't Stand So Close To Me — Sting
- Every day I love you less — Kaiser Chiefs
- I Used To Love Her — Guns & Roses
- Release Me — Engelbert Humperdinck
- Bring Your Daughter To Slaughter — Iron Maiden
- You Can't Always Get What You Want — Stones
- Suspicious Mind — Elvis Presley
- I Hate Everything About You — Three Days Grace
- Love Will Tear Us Apart — Joy Division
- Suspicious Minds — Elvis Presley
- What's Love Got To Do With It — Tina Turner

By all means, marry; if you get a good wife, you'll become happy if you get a bad one, you'll become a philosopher.

Socrates (469BC-399BC)

Greek Philosopher

Gigs Gallery

Below are the pubs/clubs that I have played in with various bands and musicians and supplied artistes for their venues in North West England. The names of the Managers/Landlords are also listed year 2008-2014.

- » Alexandra Wigan - Paul
- » Amberswood, Ince –Phil
- » Arden Arms, Bredbury-Lee/Pauline
- » Arden, Blackburn- Barbra
- » Antelope, Bolton –Mick
- » Baccarres Arms, Aspull - Martin
- » Banners, Hindley Green-Tina
- » Barnstomers, Horwich–Mark
- » Barley Corn, Chorlton cum Hardy-Elaine
- » Bay Horse, Ashton -in Makerfield –Andrew Wilkinson
- » Bay Horse, Horwich-Pat Smith
- » Bee Hive, Horwich-Lyndsey
- » Beggar & Gentleman, Barnsley-Tom
- » Britannia, Ullswater-Alan
- » Bridge Inn, Horwich-Lee &Corrine
- » Britannia, Darwen-Jackie Chadwick
- » Brooks Arms Chorley-Mike/Joanne
- » Bucks Head Abram -Donna
- » Bull & Butcher, Leigh-Kevin
- » Black Diamond, Lower Ince – Doreen

- » Blue Belle, Atherton-Brenda
- » Buckton Vale Social Club, Stalybridge-John Hulton,
- » Boathouse, Garswood – Janet Parr
- » Boathouse, Irlam – Martin/Jean
- » Bowling Green, Lancaster-Alan
- » Bowling Green, Horwich, Bolton - Nicola
- » Brook Tavern, Swinton – Chris Wheeler
- » Brown Cow, Worsley- Mary
- » Car Mill, Burnley- Lisa
- » Cardwell Arms, Adlington - Ieuan Jones
- » Cart & Horses, Astley – Carol
- » Carter Arms, Sale Moor-Liz Alcock
- » Charlestown, Blackley- Phil
- » Church Inn, Flixton – Lance Danny
- » Church Inn, Lowton –Paul Hennings
- » Comfortable Gill Glazebury- Victor
- » Coach & Horses, Cadishead -Angela
- » Commercial, West Houghton-Frank Gregory
- » Commercial, Castleton - John
- » Coppull Conservative Club, Chorley-Maurice Huyton
- » Cross, Guns, Westhoughton-Carl
- » Crown, Heaton Mersey-Tom / Joy
- » D'Havilland, Bolton/Hawkers- Malcolm
- » Deanbrook, Manchester – Rob Callum
- » Derby Arms, Hindley – Christine Donerty
- » Dog & Partridge Orrell – Nick /Jo

- » Dog & Partridge, Heaton Mersey-Kelly Robinson
- » Duke Of York Chorley - Janice
- » Duke Of York Eccles Robert Ashton
- » Dusty Miller, Bury- Julie/Steve
- » Dutton Arms, Eccles-Karl
- » Ellesmere Port Royal British Legion –J.Blake
- » Ellesmere Sports Club, Worsley – Mark Wagstaff
- » Farmers Arms, Bolton-Barry
- » Farmers Arms, Burnage, - Tony
- » Failsworth Lib Club, Failsworth – Jeanette Taylor
- » Finisher, Bolton-Dennis
- » Fleece, Ashton Makerfield-Donna
- » Flying Dutchman, Padiham– Ben Bird
- » Flixton Golf Club-Andrew Oliver
- » Folly, Swinton – Paul Oldfield
- » Gardeners Arms, Denton -Steve & Debbie
- » Gardeners, Wigan–Phil &Steph
- » Garrick, Urmston –Paul Wilson
- » Gatehouse Tlydesley – James Hewitt
- » George, Darwen- Victor Brookes
- » George & Dragon, Cheadle-Cooky/Phil
- » Gerrard Arms, Aspull -Dave
- » Glass Blower, Warrington–Ray/Bob
- » Golden Lion, Ashton Makerfield-Andy/Nicola
- » Grants, Ramsbottom- Mark
- » Green Man, Inglewhite-Karen Onder

- Greenwood Arms, Horwich-Simon Threfall
- Greyhound, Worsley- Don
- Greyhound Bolton- Stanley
- Greyhound, Glazebury - Andy
- Grove, Huddersfield- Chris Barr
- Halfway House, Royton - Andy
- Hare & Hound, Clayton Moor- Charlotte
- Hare & Hound, Golborne – George /Ann
- Hare & Hound, Aspull– Dave/Jason
- Highland Laddie, Mossley- Anita
- Hopwood, Castleton
- Hulton Arms, Westhoughton– Sharon Vine/Ian Jones
- Irlam Catholic Social Club, Irlam- Des Curran
- Irish Club, Orford- Jimmy Murray
- Jolly Falstaff, Warrington-Carol/Dan
- Kings Head, Warrington- Andy / Jay
- King William, Platt Bridge-Tracey
- Lancashire Ward Liberal, Stalybridge –Peter Smith
- Lady Lourdes Social ,Bolton
- Ladysmith, Rochdale –Colin
- Last Order, Failsworth - Mary
- Lower House Mill, Burnley-Carl
- Mechanic Arms, Hindley Green –Pip
- MacDonald Kilhey Court, Standish –Spencer Smith
- Morris Dancers, Bolton –Maureen/Colin
- Moor Top, Stockport- Peter

- Moss Vale, Urmston - Barbra
- Nelson Quarter Deck Warrington-Liam/Tony
- Netherley Royal British Legion, Liverpool -Dixie
- Newton Social, Warrington - Ste
- Oddfellows, Eccles-Carol
- Old David Inn, Alkrington-Lorraine
- Old Oak, Houghton. Preston - Aziz
- Old packet House, Broadheath- Terry Hardman
- Owd Tatts, Chadderton - Jay
- Pack Horse, Failsworth-Rachael Mickey
- Packed Horse, Failsworth – Rachael/Tom
- Pagefield, Wigan - Sharon
- Patricroft Social Club, Eccles-Tracey
- Pear Tree, Collins Green, Warrington -Steve
- Penketh Conservative, Warrington- Dennis Parker
- Piped Bull, Newton-le-Willows - Kevin
- Plough, Cadishead- Steven/Karen
- Plough Inn, Croft-Kurt
- Queens Arm, Boothtown- Mick
- Queens, Platt Bridge – Mr.Fong/ Tracey
- Queen Anne, Bolton-Stuart
- Railway Hotel, Leigh - Ian
- Railway, Huntcoat – Ian & Sarah
- Railway & Linette, Middleton-Amanda/John
- Railway, Ramsbottom-Sarah/Simon
- Red Lion, Lowton – Gareth/Peter/Kirsty

- Red Lion – Westhoughton- Adam
- Red Lion- Worsley-David
- Red Lion-Withington- Janet
- Ridgeway Arms, Adlington-Nigel King/Diane
- Rivington, Blackrod-John
- Robin Hood Ashton Makerfield -Sheila
- Rockhouse Eccles- Gary Jones
- Romiley Liberal Club, Romiley- Janet Lawson
- Rope & Anchor, Warrington-Lisa
- Rose Grove Social, Burnley-Clifford Heaton
- Rosemount, Bacup-Hilary
- Royal Arms Cadishead–Des
- Royal British Legion, Woolston Ronny/Tom Bates
- Royal Oak, Chorlton – Christine & Martin
- Rudheath Social, Rudheath –Dennis Baker
- Ryecroft, Cheadle Hulme-Russell
- St.Bonifaces Social Club, Broughton – Chris Gargan
- Sacred Heart Club, Kirby -Danny Duffy
- Sawyers Arms, Deansgate- Jess Harris
- Shanghai Palace, Wigan -Simon
- Shamrock, Ancoats-Becky/Teresa
- Shepherd's Inn – Lowton –Paul/Teresa
- Ship Inn, Rainhill -Adrian Stone
- Silver Dollar, Leigh – Terry/Linda
- Spinners Arms, Hindley, Atherton - Tony
- Springfield Chorley– Tommy

- » Staghead, Bolton-Simon
- » Stanley Road Conservative Club, Oldham Roy Burns
- » Stanley Street Social, Accrington-Phil Miller
- » Starkies Arms, Padiham- Jack/Sean/Alex
- » Stokes, Padgate-Les
- » Station Hotel, Orrell-Ray
- » Steamer Hotel, Fleetwood-Chris Barr
- » Stretford Ex-Servicemen Club–Fred McClure
- » Swan Hotel, Hindley Green -Julie / Andy
- » The Chadwick, Urmston, Philip
- » The Crown Didsbury -Tara/John
- » The Duke of Wellington Lostock - Alan Whitsun
- » The Farewell, Rochdale –Chris Holt
- » The George, Romiley- Maria & Anna
- » The Grapes –Stoneclough- Will
- » The Ivory, Urmston – Joanna Stone
- » The Lamb, Bolton -Stanley
- » The Mauldeth, Burnage-Steve & Karen
- » The Moorings, Worsley-Paul Tabbener
- » The Parrswood, Didsbury- Sharon Gaskell
- » The Park, Bryn -Marjorie
- » The Poacher, Wigan –Mandy
- » The Poacher, Blackrod-Angela/Bob
- » The Plough, Croft- Kurt
- » The Prairie, Burnley-Chris
- » The Robin Hood Lowton-Sheila

- » The Queens Accrington Mark/Ian Spedding/Dua
- » Three Crowns, Leigh-Michaella
- » Three Pidgeons, Astley Bridge-Susan Smith/Sandra
- » Throttle's Nest, Manchester
- » Traders Jack, Chorley –Mike W/Danny/Graham
- » Toybox, Blackley-Colin /Michael
- » Travellers Rest, Lowton – Andy /Michelle
- » Turf & Feathers, Warrington
- » Thomas Egerton Bolton- Rob McClintock
- » TFI Mambo, Urmston-Patrick McManus
- » Tricky's, Accrington- Richard
- » Unity Brooks, Kersley - Mandy
- » Vic & Albert, Horwich- Gary Tuite
- » Victoria, Accrington - Monty
- » Victoria, Hindley-Matt Regan
- » Victoria, Withington -Edgar
- » Vulcan, Bolton- Carl
- » Whalley Hotel, Whalley Range- Eddie Levey
- » Whiston Labour Club, Whiston – Dennis Kennedy
- » White Bull, Bilsborrow–Simon & Shirley
- » White Hart, Middleton-George
- » White Horse, Irlam - Darren
- » White Lion, Westhoughton- Chris
- » Woolpack, Stockport – Andrew Sinclair
- » Workers Club, Rochdale- Caroline
- » Yarrow Bridge, Chorley-Matt/Fiona

List of Artistes Bands & Performers of Spectrum - Ktbg Artistes Agency

Solo Artistes

- » Alan Taylor
- » Andy Keith
- » Andrew Seddon
- » Beth Anne
- » Bobby Bender
- » Chantelle Barrow
- » Claire Enfield
- » Claire Louise
- » Craig
- » David Eden
- » Dave Thomas
- » Elvin Priestley
- » Frank Forde
- » Frank Norman
- » Gael Barrie
- » Geoff Garcia
- » Geoff Nuggent
- » Garry Flanders
- » Graham Tyson
- » Ian Michael

- James Norton
- January
- Jane Frazer
- Johnny Vincent
- Jessica Stretton
- Katie O'Malley
- Kevin Dermott
- Leigh Hitch
- Louisa James
- Marcus Pinnock
- Mike Rivers
- Natasha Marie
- Olu Ember
- Pete James
- Phil Tyler
- Paul Munro
- Radha
- Sarah Kirsten
- Sharleen Kennedy
- Stacey Saunders
- Steve Brando
- Steve Hamer
- Steve Tempo
- Susan Jay
- Tia Anne
- Tony Holland
- Vicky Lea
- Wendy Dea

List of Bands, Trios & Duos Spectrum-Ktbg

- All Change at the Rock Station
- Blue Pandas - Latin jazz & Covers
- Backtrak – Sixties Music
- The Charming Beans – Comedy Group
- The Clan - Rock
- Content G - Reggae
- The Cultivators - Reggae
- Backtrak - Sixties
- Flashback - Sixties
- Night Train – Rock
- Rhythm Jets - Motown, Soul & Pop
- Route 66 - Classic Sixties
- Rocket 55 - Fifties & Sixties
- Rockin'the Blues - Blues & Rock n' Roll
- Stir Crazy - Rock

Duos & Trios

- Marcus & Kee
- Reload
- Geoff & Kee
- 2 Generations
- The Vanguards
- Venus, Jupiter & Mars

DJs & Karaokes

- Gaz Roper
- Geoff Garcia
- Matthew & Angela
- Stuart

Speciality Acts

- The Mighty Zulu Nation

Tributes

- Abba Queens
- Blues Brothers
- Elvin Priestley – Elvis Presley Tribute
- Frank Forde- Frank Sinatra Tribute
- Ian Michael – Dean Martin /George Formby
- James Norton – Neil Diamond Tribute
- Johnny Vincent – The Swinging Sixties Show
- Marcus Pinnock –Neil Diamond & Elvis Tribute
- Matthew - Roy Orbison Tribute
- Natasha Marie – Soul & Motown Tribute Show
- Paul Monro as Robbie Williams

Comedians

- *Bobby Bender*
- *Yoki Doori*

Top 10 Spectrum-ktbg Artistes

Andy Keith

James Norton

Natasha Marie & Back to Miami

Abbaqueens

Kee & Marcus

Katie O'Malley

Frank Forde   *Elvin Priestley*   *Sarah Kirsten*

Top 10 Musicians Quotes

- "To play a wrong note is insignificant;
- To play without passion is inexcusable." Ludwig Beethoven
- "One good thing about music, when it hits you, you feel no pain." BobMarly
- "The Blues are the true facts of life expressed in words and songs, inspiration, feeling, and understanding." Willie Dixon
- "I don't know anything about reading music.
- "In my line you don't have to." Elvis Presley
- "Music is spiritual. The music business is not." Van Morrison
- "My sole inspiration is a telephone call from a producer." Cole Porter
- "I love Beethoven, especially the poems." Ringo Starr
- "You don't need any brains to listen to music." Luciano Pavarotti
- "Country Music is 3 chords and the truth." Harlan Howard
- "There are two kinds of music, the good & bad,
- I play the good kind." Louis Armstrong

Top 10 Musicians Jokes

» *Why did the chicken not go for the drumming audition?*
Because he forgot to bring his drumsticks!

» *How do you know you are too old to play?*
You worry about breaking a hip than being hip.

» *What do you call a successful Musician?*
A Guy whose wife/girlfriend has two jobs.

» *What do you get when Bach falls off a horse, but has the courage to get on again and continue riding?*
Back in the saddle again!

» *What do you get when you drop a large piano on an army base?*
Flat major.

» *How do you know you are too old to gig?*
When the only 'stones' you care about are your gallbladders and kidney.

» *Why do bagpipers walk when they play?*
To get away from the noise.

» *How do you get a guitarist to play softer?*
Place a sheet of music in front of him.

» *What do you get when you throw a piano down a mineshaft?*
A flat miner.

» *Why was the piano player arrested?*
Because he got into treble.

The Top 10 Icons of England

- » The Queen
- » The Mini Car
- » James Bond 007
- » The Red Letter Box
- » The Houses of Parliament
- » Sandwich
- » Mini Skirt
- » Robin Hood
- » Cup of Tea
- » The Bull Dog

The Top 10 Red British Icons

- » Original Red Mini Motor Car
- » Little Red Miniskirt
- » Red Routemaster-London Double Decker Bus
- » The Red Telephone Box
- » London Underground Sign
- » Guards in splendid red outfits at Buckingham Palace
- » Strawberries
- » Red Mail Box
- » Red Dragon of Wales
- » Red British Budget Box

Top 10 Historic Pubs in UK

- » The Philharmonic Dining Rooms, Liverpool built 1858.
- » Eagle & Child, Oxford, 17th Century pub.
- » Old Cheshire Cheese, London.
- » Olde Trip To Jerusalem, Nottingham.
- » Crown Posade, Newcastle.
- » Haunch of Venison, Salisbury, 14th Century pub.
- » The Eagle, Cambridge.
- » Britons Protection, Manchester.
- » Café Royal, Edinburgh, built 1863.
- » The White Lion Barthomley, Cheshire.

Public houses or pubs as they are commonly called in UK dates back to Roman times (43 - 410AD).

Inns called Tabernaes were built along roman road system that allowed the weary travellers to stop for refreshments and rest.

There are close to 60,000 pubs employing over 80,000 people. (53,000 in England & Wales, 5,200 in Scotland and 1,600 in Northern Ireland).

The Red Lion is the most common name for pubs in UK.

Top 10 Pub Facts UK

Pub with the longest name in the UK.

The Old Thirteenth Cheshire Astley Volunteer Rifleman Corps Inn, Stalybridge, Greater Manchester.

Largest pub

The Regal, Wetherspoon, Cambridge.
Originally built as Regal Cinema in 1937, seating 1,300.

Smallest pub

Signal Box in Cleethorpes.
The Nutshell, Bury St Edmunds -5 metres x 2 metres.

Lowest pub

Admiral Wells, Peterborough,
9ft below sea level.

Highest pub

Tan Inn, Yorkshire Dale,
1,700 ft above sea level.

Oldest Pub

Ye Olde Trip To Jerusalem, Nottingham. Built in 1189 A.D.

Most Southerly pub

Top House, Lizard, Cornwall.

Most common pub name

The Red Lion

Strongest ale in UK

Brew Dog's Sink The Bismarck which is measured at 40% alcohol.

Britain most remote pub

The Old Forge on Inverie,
    Scotland, is 107 miles from the nearest city and has no road access.

Top 10 Stories Linked With Song Titles

Tell me what you see - The Beatles

A Woman gets on the bus with her baby.
    The bus driver says 'ugh, that's the ugliest baby I've ever seen!'

The woman walks to the rear of the bus and sits down fuming. She says to a man next to her.

'The driver just insulted me!'

The man says: 'You go up to there and tell him off. Go on, I'll hold your monkey for you.'

Caution - Bob Marley & The Wailers

A Seal walks into a club.

Ironic - Alanis Morrisette

A lorry load of tortoises crashed into a trainload of terrapins. What a Turtle Disaster.

Hit The Road Jack – Ray Charles

A Man walks into a bar with a roll of tarmac under his arms and says: 'Pint please, and one for the road.'

Up On The Roof – The Drifters

Two aerials meet on a roof –fall in love, get married. The ceremony was rubbish but the reception was brilliant.

Oh, Lucky You – The Lightning Seeds

First Guy : 'My Wife's an Angel'
   Second Guy : 'You are lucky, mine is still alive.'

I Can't Get No Satisfaction-The Rolling Stones

A Man is incomplete until he is married, after that, he is finished. Zsa Zsa Gabor

Losing your memory - Ryan Star

'Your marriage is in trouble if your wife says, "You are only interested in one thing" and you can't remember what it is.' Oscar Levant pianist/composer

Home Sweet Home – Blake Shelton

Man: I can't stop singing Green Green Grass of Home
Doc: That sounds like a Tom Jones syndrome
Man: Is it common?
Doc: It is not unusual

God Only Knows –Brian Wilson & The Beach Boys

What is the difference between God and the Conductor?
God knows. He is not the Conductor.

Top 10 Songs with names of Animals

- » A Nightingale sang in Berkeley Square – Nat King Cole
- » Baby Elephant Walk -Henry Mancini
- » I am a Tiger - Lulu
- » I am the Walrus – The Beatles
- » Monkey Man – Toots & The Maytals
- » Skippy The Bush Kangaroo – Joe Fingers RC Swaggies
- » Three Cool Cats – The Coasters / The Silver Beetles
- » Three Little Birds – Bob Marley & The Wailers
- » The Lion Sleeps Tonight - The Tokens/Karl Denver
- » White Horse - Taylor Swift

Top 10 Songs with names of People

- » Ben – Michael Jackson
- » Carrie – Cliff Richard
- » Oh Carol – Neil Sedaka
- » Sweet Caroline – Neil Diamond
- » Diana – Paul Anka

The Top Ten List

- » Hey Joe – Jimi Hendrix
- » Michelle – Paul McCartney
- » Mrs. Robinson – Simon & Garfunkel
- » Simon Says - 1910 Fruitgum Company
- » Valerie - The Zutons

Top 10 Songs with Names of Cities

- » Detroit City – Tom Jones
- » Dakota - Stereophonics
- » Do You Know The Way To San Jose - Dionne Warwick
- » Girl From Ipanema - Astrud Giberto & Stan Getz
- » I Left My Heart in San Francisco - Tony Bennett
- » I Love Paris – Ella Fitzgerald
- » Kingston Town – Bob Marley & The Wailers
- » Massachusetts – The Bee Gees
- » Streets of London - Ralph McTell
- » Viva Las Vegas – Elvis Presley

Top 10 Songs with Names of Countries

- » America – Neil Diamond
- » Blue Hawaii – Elvis Presley
- » Born in the USA – Bruce Springsteen
- » Don't Cry For Me Argentina – Julie Covington
- » England Swings – Roger Miller
- » From Russia With Love – Matt Munro
- » Mexico – James Taylor

- » Never Been To Spain – 3 Dogs Night
- » Surfin' USA - The Beach Boys
- » Woah! We're Going To Barbados –Typical Tropical

Top 10 Songs with Names of Nationalities

- » American Woman – Guess Who
- » China Girl - David Bowie
- » English Muffins & Irish Stew - Sylvia Syms
- » Jamaican Farewell – Brothers Four
- » Mexican Shuffle - Herb Alpert's Tijuana Brass
- » Norwegian Wood - The Beatles
- » Spanish Harlem – Ben E King & Rebecca Pidgeon
- » Turning Japanese – The Vapors
- » Walk Like An Egyptian - The Bangles
- » When Irish Eyes Are Smiling –Daniel O' Donnell

Top 10 Songs with Names of Fruits

- » Banana Boat Song –Harry Belafonte
- » Blue Berry Hill - Fats Domino
- » Coconut – Nillsson
- » I Heard It Through The Grapevine - Marvin Gaye
- » Lemon Tree – Peter, Paul & Mary
- » Little Green Apples –O. C. Smith
- » One Bad Apple – The Osmonds
- » Strawberry Fields – The Beatles
- » Tutti Frutti - Little Richard
- » Tangerine – Led Zeppelin

Top 10 Wonderful Music Quotes

- Family is like music, some high notes, some low notes, but always a beautiful song.
- Music is the prayer the heart sings.
- Life is a song, love is the lyrics.
- Music speaks what cannot be expressed, soothes the mind and gives it rest, heals the heart and makes it whole, flows from the heaven to the soul.
- Music is love in search of a word.
- When the pain penetrates, the music resonates.
- Music is the medicine of the mind.
- When words fail, music speaks.
- Music is my escape, it silences the world and my worries.
- Music is a more potent instrument than any other for education, because rhythm and harmony find their way into the inward places of the soul. -Plato

Top Ten Courtesy Rules in England

- Always say Please and Thank you.
- Hold the door when you open it, if there is someone walking right behind you- and especially someone with a baby.
- If English people tell you they like to invite you for a meal, don't think it will happen tomorrow.
- If they are laughing at a joke, join in and laugh along-even if you don't understand - silence is uncomfortable for them.
- If a Musician ask you to lend them a fiver, don't. Most of them are broke!

- » As mentioned in the chapter on culture shock 'Never jump the Queue'- it is sacrosanct to the English.
- » Never stroke the hair or head of a young child or offer sweets to any kid you do not know.
- » If you accidentally step on the foot of a native and he says sorry, do not be puzzled, just smile and move on –count it as your lucky day that he was trying hard to be polite –a uniquely British trait. But don't try it again!
- » If you have difficulty understanding the various accents ask them to repeat or spell the word out or use sign language. Don't try to copy their accents –they may think you are trying to be funny.
- » Never ask them how much they earn and how much their property is worth unless they volunteer the information.

Travelling to different parts of Europe, I have had the opportunity to see, hear and meet Buskers from all over the world. Bottom right photo - I joined in busking in Athens with Chairman of Bukit Kiara Properties, Kuala Lumpur, Dato Alan Tong Kok Mau. Yes, I did get some coins thrown into the hat!

Street performers in Barcelona, London Rome & Paris.- music is everywhere in Europe where the arts & creativity flourish!

Only the English could have Invented this Language

What makes the English Language so unique and at times baffling? A language spoken by 1.2 billion people around the world.

What is it like being British?

Mr.K.T.Cheong, a wise friend of mine from back home sent me this enlightening article taken from the internet.

> We'll begin with a box, and the plural is boxes,
> But the plural of ox becomes oxen, not oxes.
> One fowl is a goose, but two are called geese,
> Yet the plural of moose should never be meese.
> You may find a lone mouse or a nest full of mice,
> Yet the plural of house is houses, not hice.
>
> If the plural of man is always called men,
> Then shouldn't the plural of pan be called pen?
> If I speak of my foot and show you my feet,
> And I give you a boot, would a pair be called beet?
> If one is a tooth and a whole set are teeth,
> Why shouldn't the plural of booth be called beeth?
>
> Then one may be that, and three would be those,
> Yet hat in the plural would never be hose,
> And the plural of cat is cats, not cose.
> We speak of a brother and also of brethren,
> But though we say mother, we never say methren.
> Then the masculine pronouns are he, his and him,
> But imagine the feminine: she, shis and shim!

Let's face it – English is a crazy language.

There is no egg in eggplant nor ham in hamburger;
neither apple nor pine in pineapple.
English muffins weren't invented in England.
We take English for granted, but if we explore its paradoxes,
we find that quicksand can work slowly, boxing rings are square,
and a guinea pig is neither from Guinea nor is it a pig.
And why is it that writers write but fingers don't fing,
grocers don't groce and hammers don't ham?
Doesn't it seem crazy that you can make amends but
not one amend.
If you have a bunch of odds and ends
and get rid of all but one of them, what do you call it?

If teachers taught, why didn't preachers praught?
If a vegetarian eats vegetables, what does a humanitarian eat?
Sometimes I think all the folks who grew up speaking English
should be committed to an asylum for the verbally insane.

In what other language do people recite at a play and play
at a recital?
We ship by truck but send cargo by ship.
We have noses that run and feet that smell.
We park in a driveway and drive in a parkway.
And how can a slim chance and a fat chance be the same,
while a wise man and a wise guy are opposites?

You have to marvel at the unique lunacy of a language
in which your house can burn up as it burns
down, in which you fill in a form by filling it out,
and in which an alarm goes off by going on.
And, in closing, if Father is Pop, how come Mother's not Mop?

Being British

Being British is about driving in a German car to an Irish pub where we drink a Belgian beer. On the way home we pick up an Indian curry or a Turkish kebab. Then we sit on Swedish furniture and watch American shows on a Japanese TV.

Most of all we're very suspicious of anything foreign.

More than that, only in Britain can you get a pizza quicker than an ambulance; only in Britain do banks leave both doors open, but chain the pens to the counter; only in Britain do supermarkets make sick people walk to the back of the store to get their prescriptions, while healthy people can get their fags at the front.

We might be British, but you can't deny that we're bloody funny.

Con Te Partiro, Adios, Sayonara & Goodbye!

It has certainly been a joyful ride and a learning curve performing with British Musicians from different genres of music.

On a last note, I wish to share with you the varied personalities I have encountered and from feedback obtained.

To protect their identities and not to embarrass them, I shall name them as fruits, objects or others.

Here are some impressionable ones out of the over one hundred.

- **Apple**—very polished, shoes always shiny (told me by his wife)
- **Train**—Always late—few times 10 mins before set start.
- **Cucumber**—Very cool & collected, deliver smooth jazzy songs.
- **Colgate**—Great vocalist but has bad breath.
- **Laundry**—Always wear almost same clothes especially panes.
- **Gorilla**—Quarrelsome and has confronted patrons, when they passed negative remarks, with 'You fat . . . . , if you are so good, why don't you come up to take my place! '
- **Gaga**—Total Diva, always looking in the mirror.
- **Pies**—Very humble & does not realise how good he/she is.
- **Volcanoe**—Very hot and short tempered, easily irritated.
- **Camera Klic**k—Take to camera like duck to water. Like to pose before, whilst playing and after the gig.
- **Springboard diver**—Dive into a song effortlessly & in perfect pitch.
- **Lion**—Mr. Perfect . Knows it all, feel superior at all times.
- **Elephant**—Often forget to bring this or that except himself to gigs.
- **Headmaster**—Very strict with set and will tell you off, if you

don't toe the line. Stop on the dot and will not play another song despite pleadings from customers. ' We play 2 x 45 mins and that's it, what more do you want ?'

- » **Sweet Mandarin**—Always send me, without fail, Thank you note with the cheque and long letter describing in details how the gig went.
- » **Crutch**—Always has lots of personal problems and likes borrowing—this & that, but seldom returning.
- » **Soap**—Every few words from his mouth is peppered with the F word. I could never say it.
- » **In fact**, I can count on my fingers the number of times I have uttered it in extreme circumstances.
- » **Secret Agent**—Told me not to mention the word gigs in email or text. 'Just say 'Are you free for game of darts?' on such and such a date.

Well, these are some of the colourful characters I have met. I do my best to maintain good relationship with all and consider all of them as friends.

I wish to thank all musicians, artistes, landlords, managers, concert secretaries of pubs and clubs for all their understanding and support.

Thanks also to all Readers of my book and do email me any comments you may have.

All good wishes,
Y.B. Kee-Yeow

bienkee@yahoo.com

The Author & the Mighty Zulu Nation

www.ingramcontent.com/pod-product-compliance
Lightning Source LLC
Chambersburg PA
CBHW071450040426
42444CB00008B/1281